# 10

# MINUTE GUIDE TO

# BUSINESS COMMUNICATION

by Raymond M. Olderman

## alpha books

### Macmillan Spectrum/Alpha Books

*A Division of Macmillan General Reference*
*A Simon & Schuster Macmillan Company*
*1633 Broadway, New York, NY 10019-6705*

International Standard Book Number: 0-02-861405-4
Library of Congress Catalog Card Number: **A catalog record of this publication is available through the Library of Congress.**

99  98  97     8  7  6  5  4  3  2  1

Interpretation of the printing code: the rightmost double-digit number is the year of the book's first printing; the rightmost single-digit number is the number of the book's printing. For example, a printing code of 97-1 shows that this copy of the book was printed during the first printing of the book in 1997.

*Printed in the United States of America*

Publisher: Theresa Murtha

Editor-in-Chief: Richard J. Staron

Production Editor: Linda Seifert

Editor: Mike McFeely

Cover Designer: Dan Armstrong

Designer: Glenn Larsen

Indexer: Nadia Ibrahim

Production Team: Angela Calvert, Lori Cliburn, Maureen Hanrahan, Mary Hunt, Mindy Kuhn, Megan Wade

# CONTENTS

# INTRODUCTION

Remember the party game called "telephone?"

Several people form a circle. One person whispers a message to the next, who passes it on to the next, who passes it on...until the last person in the circle says the message out loud. Then everyone laughs at how distorted the message has become.

Imagine if this happened in the workplace.

The research and development team might set out to create a new corn plaster.

The product manager might think he has to produce a horn fastener.

The marketing department might start selling a new product called storm master.

Not possible, you say? Of course not. But something like this occurs frequently because of unskilled communications. Orders go unfilled. People miss deadlines. Bills get misdirected. Customers don't get what they expect. The business loses money or spends more than it should.

It's no joke. And it doesn't have to happen. Good communication is not hard. It just takes focus, determination, practice—and this *10 Minute Guide to Business Communication*.

Here is a quick reference list of guidelines that we'll be exploring throughout this book. Think of them as touchstones. Before you get frustrated by communication problems, repeat them to yourself—just like counting to 10 before getting angry!

Here are 10 essentials of effective communication:

1. Know your audience.
2. Respect your audience and suspend judgments.
3. Know exactly what you want to achieve.
4. Think and organize before you proceed.
5. Think from your audience's point of view.
6. Be mindful of what your face and body are conveying nonverbally.
7. Listen carefully to all responses.
8. Be willing to share what you know and hear what you don't know.
9. Stay focused on what you want to achieve and don't get distracted.
10. Find a way to get your audience to explain what they think you said. Discuss differences until you hear a satisfactory version of the message you wanted to convey.

## CONVENTIONS USED IN THIS BOOK

This book uses three icons to help you quickly find important information:

 **Timesaver Tip** Offers ideas that economize effort and avoid confusion.

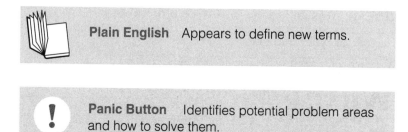

**Plain English** Appears to define new terms.

**Panic Button** Identifies potential problem areas and how to solve them.

# Acknowledgments

This book came to be because of two people: Dick Staron and John Woods. Dick, editor-in-chief at Macmillan, commissioned John Woods of CWL Publishing Enterprises to develop this book. John asked me to write it and then supported me throughout the process. I want to thank both of them. And thank you for selecting this book to help in mastering the many facets of successful business communication.

# The Author

Raymond M. Olderman is a writer, teacher, and communications consultant. He has published extensively on trends in American culture, including an award-winning book that was among the first to analyze America in the 1960s (*Beyond the Waste Land*, Yale, 1972). He left a tenured position at the University of Wisconsin in Madison in 1980 to be a professional communications consultant and writer. Since then he has conducted seminars for corporations on creativity, communications, and problem-solving. He has written business-to-business materials for almost all areas of business, industry, education, and social services. He has successfully written for theater, film, and radio and has been a practicing actor and theater director.

# COMMUNICATION: WHAT IS IT?

*In this lesson you'll learn the meaning and value of effective
communication, and its importance to you and your organization.*

## BUILDING A DEFINITION OF EFFECTIVE COMMUNICATION

Scan the activity in your organization on any given day.
Phone conversations. Memos and reports. Proposals and presentations. Gossip. Junk mail and letters. The air is thick with
communication.

When you communicate well, other people will understand
what you want to say and take the actions you expect. Let's
begin with a clear understanding of what communication is.

Communication is the process of sending and receiving messages. Effective communication:

- Achieves shared understanding.

- Stimulates others to take actions to achieve goals.

- Directs the flow of information to help people overcome barriers to open discussion.

- Channels information to encourage people to think in new ways and to act more effectively.

 **Shared Understanding**  This is the primary goal of all communication, which means that both sender and receiver understand the message and act on the message in the same way.

# COMMON FORMS OF COMMUNICATION

If you've watched television, you're familiar with mass communication. More often than not, you're simply on the receiving end of this kind of communication, so that will not be a focus of this book. Instead, this book will help you understand the following forms of communication and make you more effective when participating in each form:

- Conversational communication occurs between two or three people, and is generally very direct. You talk (send a verbal message), and receive an immediate response.

- Small group communication occurs between eight to 10 people, and remains fairly immediate, although transitions between the different message senders can become more tricky.

- Large group communication occurs in groups of roughly 10 or more. The communication may be more formalized, with a single speaker sending messages and designated time for receivers to ask questions.

Note that all these forms of communication can occur verbally, or can transpire in another way, such as via a written document, e-mail, or voice mail.

# THE POSITIVE VALUE OF GOOD COMMUNICATION

For a moment, forget what happens when information is garbled, hoarded, or badly expressed. Effective communication takes effort, and worrying about consequences won't motivate you to make the effort. Concentrate instead on all the good reasons to work on your skills.

Effective communication helps you: anticipate problems, make decisions, coordinate workflow, supervise others, develop relationships, and promote products and services.

When you communicate effectively you sort out relevant data from a huge amount of available input and convey only what helps your audience take productive action. You turn data into information that has clear meaning and relevance to your audience.

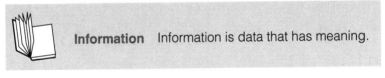

**Information**    Information is data that has meaning.

Finally, remember, effective communication helps you help your organization because it promotes shared information and also promotes teamwork and increased productivity.

**Productivity**    Productivity is the ratio of cost to output. Increased productivity means it costs less to produce the same or more, thus resulting in higher profits.

In this lesson you learned the meaning and value of effective communication, and its importance to you and your organization. The next lesson introduces the communication process.

# UNDERSTANDING THE COMMUNICATION PROCESS

*In this lesson you will learn the basic model or flow of the communication process. You will also examine real-world complications that make successful communication a challenge.*

## THE BASIC COMMUNICATION MODEL

In an ideal world, communication involves these simple components:

1. A sender, who is the person initiating the communication, or broadcasting the message.

2. A message, the specific set of words, gestures, and images that the sender uses to convey what he or she wants to say.

3. A channel, through which the message moves.

4. A receiver or receivers, or the audience for the message, from whom the receiver often expects a response.

5. Feedback, which is the response from the receiver to the sender.

# COMMUNICATION INTERFERENCE

In the real world, noise interferes with every message, complicating its flow through the communication model. If you understand the communication model, you can take the time to think about noise that may interfere with your message at various points, anticipate that noise, and take extra precautions to ensure your message arrives intact.

## SENDER COMPLICATIONS

You don't store away information like objects of inventory placed in a box or put on a shelf. It's necessary for you to be aware of how your internal frameworks and filters interpret and convert data, knowledge, and facts into information and messages. If you are not aware, the messages you send out may not be what you think they are.

**Internal Frameworks**   Your internal frameworks are the limits you put around any input, data, or stimulus so that it makes sense to you.

**Internal Filters**   Your internal filters are your automatic habits of excluding any input, data, or stimulus that is outside what you have learned to believe based on your experience.

Filters and frameworks can be like prejudices. They can make you hear only what you want to hear. Filters and frameworks also keep you from communicating anything except what confirms your opinions. If you think laziness is your problem with productivity, you won't consider any new ideas for dealing with the situation. You'll just tell your staff to work harder because that's consistent with your framework.

Unexamined frameworks and filters can make your messages sound repetitious, and give the impression that you're inflexible. In addition, your personal communication style—how forceful or meek you seem, for example—can affect how your message is interpreted.

## MESSAGE COMPLICATIONS

The content of your message cannot be something that simply comes to mind. You must deal with the complications of determining the accuracy and value of your content, both in terms of how you think your audience will respond to it, and in terms of whether it suits your goals for the message.

If the content of your message is ambiguous or inappropriate, you must look for every way to reduce the possibility of misinterpretation.

## CHANNEL COMPLICATIONS

The channel you choose can affect whether your receiver understands your message as you intended, or whether the message is received in a timely fashion. There are three different channel complications:

1. You have to choose among many channels and find the right one. Possible formal and informal channels include:

- Talk channels such as: the telephone, face-to-face conversation, speeches, or meetings.

- Written channels such as: letters, memos, reports, proposals, electronic mail, promotions, advertising, and public relations.

2. Many things can interfere with the flow of your message and its clarity. Here are some examples of channel interference: Noise from the surrounding area, time of day, failure in the channel (such as messages lost in the mail or in a network), and speed of the channel.

3. Be aware of the complications to your message caused by the direction the message must travel. One thing that affects what you say in your message is whether it's aimed at superiors, subordinates, or peers. Be more formal or less formal depending on the direction of your message.

## RECEIVER COMPLICATIONS

The receiver, just like the sender, has frameworks and filters for interpreting messages. You can be certain that the receiver's frameworks and filters will differ from the sender's, due to cultural differences, state of mind and health, company values, or communication style. The differences complicate the process of communication, reinforcing the need for clarity.

Therefore, before actually sending your message, you need to look at the noise that the receiver brings to the process, and adjust the message accordingly.

## FEEDBACK COMPLICATIONS

Both sender and receiver must actively seek clarity in their communications. When the receiver of your message provides feedback, you'll know whether the receiver has interpreted the message as intended. However, if feedback is angry, ambiguous, or nonexistent, it introduces even more noise into the communication process, making shared understanding an even more difficult goal to achieve.

In this lesson you learned the mechanics of how the communication process works and how to identify the complications that occur in real-world communications. The next lesson helps you define the goal for your message.

# 3

# DEFINE YOUR GOAL AND APPROACH

*This lesson helps you define the goal for a message and understand how that goal may have an impact on the content of your message.*

## YOUR COMMUNICATION ASSIGNMENT

In many communication situations, you send a message, un-prompted, because it's a normal part of your job. For example, you might prepare and send a weekly report to several people or your boss might ask you to handle a particular communication task, such as following up with a vendor or another department in your company.

In either case, you usually are aware of what your assignment is, and what the basic content of your message might be. However, those pieces of information aren't enough to ensure that your communication will be successful. Before you broadcast the message, you'll need to analyze the specific goal of the message, the receiver, the channel to send it over, and even yourself as sender.

# IDENTIFYING YOUR GOAL OR PURPOSE

Every message you send will have one or more of the following four goals:

- **To inform.** You might need to communicate key information or statistics, such as the result of a customer survey or the outcome of product testing. With this communication goal, you're providing information for use in decision-making, but aren't necessarily advocating a course of action.

- **To request.** Messages that make a request ask for a specific action by the receiver. Requests may be simple or complex.

- **To persuade**. Persuasive messages are intended to reinforce or change a receiver's belief about a topic. In some cases, you may also want the receiver to act on the belief.

- **To build relationships.** This goal is often overlooked in business communication. Some messages you send may have the simple goal of building goodwill between you and the receiver.

# UNDERSTANDING HOW YOUR GOAL AFFECTS YOUR MESSAGE

Before you develop or send any message, you should first take the time to identify which goal or goals you want to accomplish with the message. Understanding the goal will help you identify what kind of information, and how much information, the message should include. While there are any number of ways in which a goal can affect message content, here are a few examples:

- When you're informing a receiver who's part of your organization about the current status of a project, you can probably just list a few key points. However, if you're briefing a new consultant who'll be helping out with the project, you'll need to provide more background information.

- When you're requesting a receiver to do something new or something that's complicated, you'll need to be sure your message contains enough details about the steps the receiver should take, and contains all the information the receiver needs to complete your request.

- When you're trying to persuade a receiver about an issue, you need to be sure to provide ample rationale for your position. For example, while a statement like "The president of the company says we have to change this approach" does obligate employees to respond accordingly, such a simple statement may not be enough to help the employees really accept and support the change.

- If your goal is to build a relationship, analyze the type of relationship you'd like to build, and structure your messages accordingly. For example, if your business has 20 clients, but only four of those clients provide 80 percent of your revenue, you should spend much more time with follow-up for those four clients, and regularly reinforce that you appreciate the significant business each client provides.

In this lesson, you learned how to identify the goal for your message. The next lesson will cover how to analyze the receiver of the message.

# TAKING A LOOK
## AT YOUR
## AUDIENCE

*In this lesson you will learn how to analyze your audience and how
to get its attention so you can create an effective message. You'll
also learn how to deal with special audience circumstances.*

## DID I JUST SAY THE WRONG THING?

Imagine your embarrassment if you prepared remarks on marketing and discovered you had an audience of engineers. Even
worse, you could have an audience of marketers and still not
reach them. You could be talking about a technique they just
used without success.

Whether your audience is a single individual, a team, or a
large group, the more you know about it, the better your
chance of reaching it.

## HOW TO ANALYZE YOUR AUDIENCE

Ask yourself the following questions and write down your
answers.

1. Who exactly is your audience?

   • What do you know about their habits of listening, their personality quirks, their age, and related areas of interest?

   • Are they defensive, self-conscious, easily offended, formal, or informal?

   • Are there any cultural differences you need to make adjustments for?

2. What does your audience know about the subject of your message?

3. What does your audience need to know?

4. Does your audience need to have technical knowledge to pay attention to your message?

5. Does your audience have a preconceived attitude toward your information? Is it positive or negative?

6. What is your relationship to your audience? Is it friendly, formal, or perhaps even hostile?

7. What recent events or circumstances has your audience experienced that could be relevant to the subject of your message?

8. What action do you want your audience to take?

## THE MOST IMPORTANT RULE FOR REACHING YOUR AUDIENCE

Take your audience's point of view. When you put yourself in an audience member's shoes, you get a clearer idea of what elements will make your message effective. Communication experts call this developing the "you attitude."

# SOME GUIDELINES FOR TARGETING YOUR AUDIENCE

Once you've developed a clear picture of your audience's thoughts, feelings, and potential responses to a message, you can begin to develop specific strategies for appealing to the audience and getting its attention. Here are some targeting techniques that you can apply to your message:

- Pay attention to the environment in which you will deliver your message and the time of day. If you'll be speaking after lunch, for example, the audience might be sleepy, so your talk will need to be very lively, or perhaps interactive.

- Organize your message to take account of what you know about the personalities and sensitivities of your audience.

- Build your message in steps, moving toward the more controversial elements.

- Avoid information overload.

- Anticipate objections, and plan your responses, and look for ways to build support for your position.

- Focus on what is positive and give it emphasis.

- Provide room for feedback by making it clear that you want it and that there will be no negative consequences for those who provide it.

# WHAT TO DO WHEN YOUR AUDIENCE IS NOT RECEPTIVE

Here are some strategies to use if your audience is not receptive to what you have to say:

- Begin with areas of agreement. If you know your audience disagrees with your approach to increasing sales, begin with a checklist of standard approaches. Find out which ones you both agree are applicable to your situation. If you still believe your approach is correct, show your audience how it might better accomplish the same goals as the approach your listener has in mind.

- Eliminate ambiguity. This way there is no room for your audience to pounce on an unsympathetic interpretation.

- Stay away from flash points. If you know your audience doesn't like having the sales staff fill out forms to gather data on existing clients, don't try to introduce a new form by saying: "I've developed a form for keeping track of your client's preferences and buying habits."

 **Flash Point**   A flash point is a subject or point-of-view that is controversial and very likely to make your audience respond negatively.

- Stay away from unnecessarily provocative statements.

 **Provocative Statement**   A provocative statement is not just a controversial one—it's a statement *intended* to make your audience have a strong reaction. Provocative statements can be useful when you're trying to inform or persuade, as long as the provocation relates clearly to the message and doesn't appear to attack a person or group.

- Be realistic about the expected results of any change or solution you propose. Offer a solution as a good way to deal with the immediate needs.

## WHAT TO DO WHEN YOU ARE MAKING HEAVY DEMANDS ON YOUR AUDIENCE

A reliable understanding of your audience can help you avoid unnecessary challenges to their knowledge, their norms, or their powers of concentration. Here are some steps you can take when the challenges are unavoidable:

1. Organize difficult material or requests in checklists so your audience can proceed step by step.

2. Provide materials that make it easier to understand and act on your message—forms, outlines, addressed envelopes, guidelines, definitions of terms.

3. Tell them how they will benefit, so that their efforts will have a payoff. Put benefits first.

4. Keep a friendly and helpful tone, but don't be condescending.

5. Don't reveal any impatience. When you feel it coming on, go back to any point of shared understanding or agreement.

6. Use clear, everyday language as much as possible. Avoid emotional terms such as political labels or other language that may refer to religious or ethnic issues.

7. Use anecdotes to illustrate difficult to understand material, and don't fall into lecturing or repeating phrases such as "Do you follow?" or "Do you know what I mean?" that can make people feel uncomfortable.

8. Don't refer to other documents or memos from past correspondence without offering reminders and summaries of what those said.

## DEALING WITH SEVERAL AUDIENCES AT ONCE

If your message goes to multiple audiences, analyze the role each audience segment plays. Here are some questions you can ask:

- Is there a primary receiver? Who is the decision maker? The primary receiver is the person you're directly addressing. This person may be different from a decision maker who has final say over a request or approval of an idea.

- Are there secondary audiences who must concur with the primary audience for your message to succeed? A secondary audience might include other colleagues who will be affected by what you are suggesting.

- Is there a screener who you must get past to reach your primary audience? A screener might be a secretary or someone else who sees your message before the person to whom it is addressed. A screener needs to be able to quickly see what the message is about and determine its importance to the person you've sent it to.

In this lesson you learned how to analyze your audience, how to get their attention, and how to deal with special audience circumstances. In the next lesson, you can look at how and when to deliver your message.

# CHOOSING THE RIGHT CHANNEL AND THE RIGHT TIME

*In this lesson you'll learn how to identify the most useful channel
and timing to suit your message goal and audience.*

## WHY A THOUGHTFUL APPROACH PAYS

In business, choosing the wrong channel or mistiming a communication can cause an immediate loss of advancement,
progress, sales, or profits.

Unless you're brainstorming in a creative session, it usually
pays to stop and think about the right way to say what you
have in mind. And the right time to say it.

## HOW TO SEND A MESSAGE

Should your message be spoken, written, or a combination of
the two? Primary speaking channels include the telephone,
face-to-face conversation, speeches, presentations, and meetings. The written channels you're most likely to use include
letters, memos, reports, proposals, and electronic mail.

Each channel has its unique benefits and characteristics. For example, written messages (unless they're handwritten) are generally more formal, there's usually a delay between when you send the message and when it's received. Spoken channels, such as a phone call can be informal. Presentations or situations like job interviews require a more careful communication approach.

## WHAT DO YOU NEED FROM THE CHANNEL?

You need to examine which channel will help you reach your message goal and will be most appropriate for your audience. Here are several criteria that will give you the information you need to choose a channel:

1. What channel best serves the goal of the message? Some channels are quite obviously inappropriate for a particular message.

2. How urgent is this message? Is it urgent for the sake of business? And is it urgent to you personally? If the message is urgent because it's crucial to the success of your team or business, or because the message must be sent so that the receiver(s) can act on the message by a particular deadline, consider a channel that's very timely, such as a phone call or e-mail. If the message is urgent to you personally—say, you have a deadline but need help to complete the task—you may want to start out with a different channel, such as a memo.

3. Do you need to document the message in some way? If you deliver a message verbally, such as via a phone call, you can follow up with a confirming note, just to ensure that the common understanding between you and your receiver is on the record.

4. How complex or specialized will the message content be? Ask yourself the following about your message:

   - Is the message long and/or complicated, or does it describe a process or project that is?

   - Should the message be made confidential?

   - Should you add some supporting materials to help make the message more complete?

5. What communication channel does the receiver expect or prefer? If your message purpose is anything other than routine, give thought to the personality, preferences, knowledge, and situation of your audience members. Some people prefer a phone call or meeting, due to the more personal feel of such channels.

6. In what direction is the message going? Consider what you know about the company norms for communicating with peers, subordinates, and superiors.

7. Do you want feedback? Do you want to know what your audience thinks, or whether there are misunderstandings? In such a case, a face-to-face meeting may be called for. Do you want to know what you need to do next? You could ask such a question in a brief phone message. Or, do you just have an announcement to make? A memo or e-mail message might do the trick in such a case.

## Choosing the Right Channel

Now, you've identified what you need from the channel. Next you can select the channel that best serves your message and audience needs.

Spoken messages are spontaneous, personal, bimodal (verbal and nonverbal at the same time), immediate, and leave no record. Spoken messages are your best choice when:

- You're communicating a nonroutine or ambiguous matter.
- You're communicating an urgent matter.
- You want immediate feedback.
- You want interaction, to be sure your message is clear.
- There's an emotional component to your message that you want to communicate via nonverbal cues, such as your facial expression.
- You believe your audience will be receptive to your message.
- You don't need an exact record of your message and interaction.

Written messages allow more control, mechanical efficiency, and convenience for both sender and receiver. They provide a record. Written communications can be personal or impersonal. E-mail is the most informal channel for writing and is often one of the quickest. Written messages are your best choice when:

- You're communicating a routine matter.
- You're not worried about urgency or ambiguity.
- You need or want a documented record.
- You're communicating complex and/or numerical information.
- You want to give your receiver time to deal with the message at his or her convenience.
- You need the most economical way to reach a large and/or geographically dispersed audience.

- Your audience may not be receptive to your message, so you want a nonconfrontational, formal way to deliver the message.

- You need time to make your message clear and effective.

> **tip**
>
> **Combine Channels**   If your receiver might be closed or unreceptive to your message, consider a combination of speaking and writing. You could write a memo *and* deliver it personally. Your enthusiasm and professional presentation could be just what's needed to get approval.

## TIME YOUR MESSAGE FOR THE BEST POSSIBLE IMPACT

You can reduce or eliminate noise (complications) in your channel by choosing the best time to deliver your message.

Unless the content or urgency of your message make immediate delivery necessary, here are the major timing factors to consider when choosing when to deliver your message:

1. Other events or activities competing for attention. Is it "salesperson award day" or "sweatshirt day?" Be aware of potential distractions.

2. The prevailing organizational climate and mood. Is this a grim time? A tight-discipline time?  Time your message to complement the mood.

3. The personal circumstances of the receiver(s). Did your boss just get called down for a bad decision? Is he/she distracted by a personal matter?

4. Current work demands. Is it a peak period, a slump, a period of process improvement?

5. Frequency and spacing of the same message. Be strategic about when and how often you send the same message.

In this lesson you learned how to identify the most useful channel to suit your message and audience, and the right time to send your message. Next, you will prepare to create the message.

# RESEARCH AND PREPARATION

*In this lesson, you will learn the essential steps you should take to ensure your message is accurate and well-prepared.*

## GATHER THE FACTS

If your message has errors or mistakes, it can confuse your receiver, or cause a reaction other than the one you desired. Errors and omissions can damage your credibility, making receivers more skeptical of messages you send later. Even worse, if you make a mistake or leave out a key piece of information, you could easily lose control of a meeting or presentation, as audience members challenge your statistics or offer opposing viewpoints.

Always take steps to double-check your content, either by reviewing company statistics, checking a company database, or checking previous project records. Don't forget to check facts thoroughly, using tactics like these:

- If you need a fact or quote from a vendor or another department, get it in writing and review it in detail for missing elements.

- Take advantage of the Internet and online services, which offer databases of information, which you can use to confirm demographics, verify that you're quoting a resource accurately, or find other expert opinions that support or reinforce your message.

- If there are opposing facts or viewpoints, make sure you're aware of them or understand them.

- Have another person check the facts. It never hurts to have a colleague or assistant confirm your data or check your math.

- Tap into other experts. If you know someone who has the facts you might need, ask for them.

*tip*    **Get Organized**   If you're working with someone who's helping you gather or check facts, make sure your requests are organized.

## TOOLS TO MAKE SURE YOUR MESSAGE IS CLEAR AND PRECISE

After you've drafted your message's content, you need to refine it with the time and resources you're allowed. Clearly, it's not reasonable to spend three days repeatedly rewriting a memo that announces a company picnic. However, if you need to lead a meeting and inform your team that salary increases will be small in the company this year because your company's struggling, you shouldn't just wing it.

While in general you should allow yourself proportionally more time to write and review messages as they become more important, at the very least, you should use the following steps to refine the message and eliminate errors:

1. Once is not enough. Virtually no one can write a perfect, compelling message the first time. Be realistic, and allow yourself time for at least a second draft.

2. Time allowing, prepare the message, then set it aside for an hour or a day or two before revising it. You'll be coming back to it with a fresh eye, which may yield ideas for better phrasing or a more effective approach.

3. Always check spelling! Even though you may think that spell-checking is essential only for written documents, you should also check your presentation text, because a typo or grammar error could cause you to trip up in your delivery.

4. Always proofread your messages. Better yet, have someone else proofread them. Spell checkers don't know whether you've used the word "too" correctly in the context of a sentence (what if you meant "two"), or can't tell if you've transposed words.

*tip*  **Catch Those Errors**   A couple of proofreading tricks can help you catch errors. Try looking at the document upside-down; for some reason, this position makes typos stand out. Also, try reading sentences from the last word to the first word. This forces you to concentrate more on the spelling of each word.

# REVIEW AND REHEARSE

Even though reviewing and rehearsing may seem like an unnecessary step given the time pressures of the typical workplace, perfect preparation sets you apart from the crowd and helps your messages have greater impact.

> **!** **Rehearse** Never deliver a presentation without rehearsing it. Until you say a phrase out loud, you won't know how it sounds to an audience, or whether you can even say it without tripping up.

> **tip** **Record Your Rehearsal** Your video camera or cassette recorder can be your best friend. Record yourself as you rehearse, then watch or listen to your performance. You may find that you use an odd gesture or say "um" after every sentence. If so, you can work to eliminate those distractions from your presentation.

This lesson reviewed critical steps to prepare your message for final delivery. The next several lessons present specific writing help that you can apply to different types of messages.

# SOME BASICS OF GOOD BUSINESS WRITING

*In this lesson you will learn what good business writing is, plus fourteen guidelines to help you write well.*

## FORGET ABOUT YOUR ENGLISH TEACHER

Good business writing accomplishes the writer's goals, simply and clearly. Business writing is for practical purposes, not creative satisfaction or self-expression.

There's no reason for fear, because you don't need a writer's talent to be good at business writing. It's a skill you can learn, just like any other skill where you start with the basics and keep practicing until you do it well.

## FOURTEEN GUIDELINES FOR GOOD BUSINESS WRITING

Following several basic rules can help keep your writing on the right path, so your messages are more successful. Here are 14 guidelines you can use to become a better business writer:

1. Know your audience, what they expect, and what you want them to understand.

2. Unless you're writing a formal document, write to the audience as if you were carrying on a conversation. Although writing is not exactly like talking, you need to create that impression. Think of it as a serious conversation where you use contractions and common language. In addition to making it easier for your audience to get involved, thinking of your writing as a conversation puts you at ease and gets rid of unnecessary jitters.

3. Know your material. Most poor business writing comes from sloppy thinking. If you're explaining why your product is better than the competition, you need to know a great deal about both products. Then you can be persuasive and specific.

4. Get right to the point with as few words as possible. Make your first sentence lead directly to the point you want to make. Get rid of wordiness and redundancies. For example, instead of "at this point in time," say "at this time," or simply "now."

5. Aim for clarity at all times. Get rid of long or unusual words where short and familiar words are just as good. Avoid arty expressions. Your goal is to make your writing so clear it is transparent and your readers can see straight through to your meaning. You don't want them to notice how you write. They should be drawn to what you are saying.

6. Keep an even tone. Even if you are arguing a point, be respectful and courteous.

7. Don't make mistakes in spelling, grammar, or punctuation. People can't help but make unfavorable judgments about you if you make mistakes.

8. Learn the rules of standard usage. For example, learn when to use affect or effect, which or that, lie or lay, good or well.

9. Make conservative word choices. Stick to the norms. Avoid using old-fashioned words or new and hip ones unless you know your audience is receptive to one or the other.

10. Learn and use the following techniques for dynamic writing:

   - Use active voice instead of passive. For example, say, "I wrote the report, and then sent it to the client" rather than, "The report was written, and was then sent to the client." In most cases, no one is the actor in a passive voice sentence. Consequently, people frequently use the passive voice to conceal responsibility. This can be useful if you are dealing with sensitive staff members and don't want to place the blame on anyone in particular. Passive voice can also be useful for certain kinds of emphasis: "The report was mailed on Monday." The emphasis is on the report and the date it was mailed, not on who mailed it. In almost all other cases, passive voice will weigh down your writing. It will take the action out of your sentences.

   - Use action verbs instead of being verbs. For example, it's more interesting to say, "You can wallop this product and it won't break," than "This is a durable product and is good for hard use."

   - Use concrete nouns and verbs instead of vague ones that depend on adjectives and adverbs. For example, this is concrete: "The rotary model can pump six gallons in three minutes. Use it when you need rapid removal." This is vague: "Our very high-quality rotary model has an unusually productive output and is excellent for use in a broad range of demanding situations."

11. Avoid using strings of nouns as adjectives. For example: Don't say, "This communication project situation objective is in need of an executive process of decision making." Try saying, "To define the immediate objectives of our communication project we need some executive decisions."

12. Guide your reader. Make sure your ideas connect and that one flows into the next. Use paragraph breaks to start a new but connected line of thought. For longer documents, use brief headings as signposts to begin a new direction. Be conscious of using other signposts throughout your document. For example, repeat ideas; use italic, bold, or underlining for emphasis; tell your reader what comes next and how it relates to your overall document; use connector words such as "therefore," "in addition," or "for example."

> **!**  **Keep Things Simple**  Never let your reader do the work of making your connections. Don't refer to things that came before unless there's only a gap of one or two sentences. Remind the reader of what you're referring to.

13. Avoid stereotypes and clichés because they are offensive and carry very little information. Avoid technical language and specialized jargon unless your audience fully shares your knowledge of these insider's words.

> **Being Gender Free**   Since the 1970s, writers have made an effort not to use the male pronoun when they aren't talking about men in particular. One way to avoid the problem is to use the plural form whenever possible. For example instead of saying "The manager should not insult his staff," say "Managers should not insult staff members."

14. Vary your sentence structure and length. But do so only when it doesn't result in awkward, hard-to-follow wording. Remember the basic sentence in English has a very simple structure. Subject first, and then what the subject is doing. For example, "I walk down the street." Whenever you have a problem sentence, go back to this pattern. Don't try to fix your old sentence. Start again and keep it simple.

> *tip*   **Make A Request**   In your business writing, learn a lesson from sales people, who are trained to always ask for the order. That is, if you want your message receiver to perform a specific action as a result of your message, make your request in a clear, direct way.

In this lesson you learned what good business writing is, plus fourteen basic guidelines that will help you improve your writing. In the next several lessons, you will take a look at how to write specific types of messages.

# EFFECTIVE USE
# OF E-MAIL

*In this lesson you will learn how to create messages that use e-mail to its best advantage.*

## A NEW CHANNEL OF COMMUNICATION, A NEW CHOICE

It's useful to remember that e-mail (electronic mail) is a channel of communication—just as the telephone, and letters are. And like these other media, e-mail has strengths and weaknesses.

**E-Mail** E-mail, or electronic mail, is the medium of communication that sends and receives messages by computer over network cables and phone lines. It is used within organizations through specially designed internal networks.

## TAKE ADVANTAGE OF E-MAIL'S STRENGTHS

Speed is the major advantage of using e-mail. Just enter the names and electronic addresses of the people you want to reach, click your mouse on the send button, and your message goes to anybody or everybody you've named. Here are some other advantages:

- The cost per message is just about unbeatable.

- People who use e-mail generally feel freer, less guarded, less formal, and less intimidated by status. The medium seems to promote easier upward communication to superiors.

- Because you write e-mail messages on a computer, you have the opportunity to correct and reshape them with ease before sending.

- You can also print a copy and store your messages for future reference.

- On group projects, you can send whole files to speed up the editing process.

- You can also send any given message to as many people as you want faster and with fewer repetitive, time-wasting steps than in any other medium.

## SUIT YOUR MESSAGE TO THE MEDIUM

If you use e-mail at your workplace, you should find out your organization's established conventions and follow them. You should also find out what kinds of messages your organization considers appropriate for the company e-mail system.

In just about all cases, you should assume your messages are not confidential. They can be sent to more people than you intend and they are preserved for much longer than you realize.

This lack of confidentiality, along with the normal ethics of on-the-job behavior, dictates certain guidelines for the appropriate use of workplace e-mail:

- Don't use it to send or receive personal messages.

- Don't say things you would not want made public.

- Don't send information that is confidential, insulting, or slanderous.

- Don't use it for political petitions or individual private gain.

- Don't use it to disclose organizational business that is normally not disclosed.

# EFFECTIVE WRITING PRACTICES FOR E-MAIL

E-mail systems provide you with a ready-made format similar to the standard memo format. A well-worded subject line is even more important than in a memo because the format limits the number of words you can use. Make your subject line short, snappy, and descriptive. The goal is to let your audience know immediately what is covered in your message.

Some experts recommend that you summarize your most important point in the subject line. That's fine if your most important point also reveals the overall thrust of your message. If not, choose words that more clearly describe that thrust.

Here are some tested writing practices that make for effective e-mail messages:

- Make thoughtful use of the existing format.

- Keep the computer screen in mind when you write so you can make your message easy to read. Break up paragraphs and keep them short.

- Don't let the "quick-note" feeling of e-mail lure you into shooting off memos without proofreading and thinking twice about what you say.

- E-mail is not suited to complex messages. Keep the content basic.

## E-MAIL ETIQUETTE (SOMETIMES CALLED "NETIQUETTE")

You are all alone with your computer when you send out an e-mail message, and e-mail is so fast, so easy that you might forget someone will be looking once the message is sent.

- Keep messages short. Think of e-mail as a kind of telegram; too many words are costly. They cost your reader's attention.

- Watch your tone. Users consistently report that e-mail flattens tone, perhaps because the receiver isn't getting other cues about the message from your vocal tone, facial expressions, or gestures. Messages can sound angry, sarcastic, happy, or mean without the writer realizing it. If you do want to include an emotional component of your message, say it directly: "I'm angry that the brochure will not be shipped in time," or "This is a sad message for me."

**For Veterans Only**   Veteran e-mail users have created a set of symbols that represent emotion. Tilt your head sideways to the left and look at this symbol :-) It means "smile." This one :-( means "frown." These are called *smileys* or *emoticons*. If you use them, do it sparingly. They can make you look silly. Be sure you know your readers.

- Don't right-justify or use all capital letters. In fact, all capital letters represents SCREAMING in e-mail, and can cause a hostile reaction. If you want to emphasize a word, insert an asterisk before and after it, as in: "We *really* need to hit this deadline."

- Don't get too informal. Use standard English and think of it as relaxed rather than informal.

- Check your mail frequently. This piece of etiquette is the most frequently mentioned request. If you don't check your e-mail, the entire purpose of a quick action note is defeated.

In this lesson you learned how to create messages that use the e-mail medium to the best advantage. The next lesson covers written messages that inform the receiver.

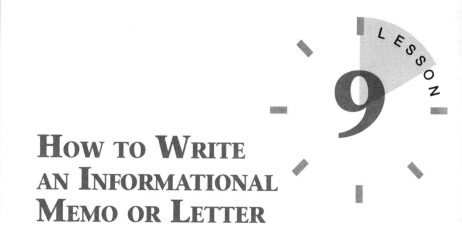

# HOW TO WRITE AN INFORMATIONAL MEMO OR LETTER

*In this lesson you will learn guidelines and formats for writing effective informational memos and letters.*

## FIVE REASONS FOR AN INFORMATIONAL MEMO OR LETTER

Business letters and memos differ primarily in format and destination. In almost all cases, letters are communications that go outside your organization; are communications that travel within the organization. You might use a letter inside your organization if you need to deal with highly sensitive or confidential personnel matters, or if the practice is an established courtesy. Overall, there are five reasons why you might need to write an informational memo or letter:

1. Making an inquiry or request for information.
2. Responding to requested information.
3. Making a recommendation.
4. Providing notification of changes that are not negative.
5. Providing information for the record.

# Five Guidelines for Effective Informational Memos and Letters

Don't "dash off" your memos and letters. Practice the same principles of good communication (such as knowing your audience and keeping it brief) discussed throughout this book. They are your starting point for writing effective memos and letters. In addition to using the general guidelines you've already learned, you should practice the following techniques to improve the effectiveness of your informational letters and memos:

1. Double-check the accuracy of any information you intend to convey.

2. Double-check the content of any memo or letter you are responding to.

3. Be direct and save the reader time. If you're asking for information, put your request in the first sentence.

4. Use the appropriate heading and format for a memo or letter. See "Sample Documents," later in this lesson.

5. Use the following basic structure for the main body of your memo or letter:

   - Begin with your main point, and make it important to your reader.

   - Follow with well-organized details and explanations.

   - Close with a request for action or friendly comment for goodwill.

 **Don't Beg for Questions**   Unless the information in your memo or letter is complex, avoid using such standard wording as "Feel free to call for more information." In most cases the information you provide should be all they need.

## SAMPLE DOCUMENTS

The following examples can serve as models for informational memos and letters that you create. Figure 9.1 shows a standard business memo.

In Figure 9.1, the date is necessary to compile a record and to inform the receiver of the currency of the memo. The subject should be to the point and if possible include the writer's angle on the subject. The body text of the memo should be logically ordered just as in a letter. The tone should be conversational if possible. The close, or final paragraph of the memo, should ask for some kind of action.

Figure 9.2 provides an example of an inquiry letter.

---

MEMO
DATE:       June 29, 1996
TO:         Mavis Anderson
FROM:       Tom Leske
SUBJECT: Recommended computer changes in your
            department

Could you please review the attached report and let me know how you feel about the recommended hardware and software changes?

As you know, we have proposed several changes to accommodate our new accounts. I'd like to know by Friday if you think these changes will assist production in your area.

Can you estimate the time you'll need for training? Do you foresee any problems with staff resistance?

Mavis, don't be reluctant to let me know your real opinion of what we have proposed. We want this to help production in your department. If you don't think it will, tell me now.

---

Figure 9.1    A standard business memo.

You'll notice that in Figure 9.2, the opening paragraph asks direct questions that go to the heart of the matter. The receiver knows instantly if the letter is relevant to her company.

The body text is organized to progress from finding out if the company supplies what the writer needs, to supplying basic details about the writer's needs facilitating a useful response, to informing the receiver of what actions to take.

Figure 9.3 is a response to an inquiry.

---

Empty Acres Metropolitan School District
1887 Bolling Avenue, Cool Crest, WY 81281
808/274-9978

June 30, 1996
Janis Wild, President
Wild-One's Good Idea Service
144 5th Avenue
New York, NY 10022
Dear Ms. Wild:

Do you supply ideas for educational video scripts? I know of your reputation through a local playwright. It sounds as if you have the range, but can you work with prescribed outcomes? With a basic outline of contents?

We need an organizational concept for presenting thematic information to nine- and ten-year olds. We have a budget and a fairly firm deadline of March 30, 1997.

Are you interested?

If you are, please send me information on your services, rates, and a description of how you work. Would you supply a proposal describing recommended concepts? Would your final presentation include a description of how to put the selected concept into a workable script?

I'll get back to you with more information on our needs once I see your materials. If you need more input to help you provide us with a preliminary response, please call. I'll be happy to talk with you.

Sincerely,

Warren Methodyne, School Program Coordinator

---

Figure 9.2    A successful inquiry letter.

Wild-One's Good Idea Service
144 5th Avenue, New York, NY 10022
(212) 777-1111 Fax: 212/727-1111

July 5, 1996
Warren Methodyne, School Program Coordinator
Empty Acres Metropolitan School District
1887 Bolling Avenue
Cool Crest, WY 81281

Dear Mr. Methodyne:
I was delighted to get your letter. It would be stimulating and rewarding to work with your school district, and our organization can meet and exceed your expectations on this project.

As you requested, I've enclosed our standard description of rates and services as well as our normal development process. I need to know more details to give you a precise estimate of costs, but I am sure we can jointly figure out a way to work within your budget.

As you'll see in our materials, we do supply proposed concepts, usually two or three alternatives. Also, to answer your other question, we help clients put our concepts into production as a standard service.

We're excited about the possibility of working on an organizational concept for presenting mathematical information to nine- and ten-year olds.

Please tell me if you know enough about us to take the next step, because I really look forward to hearing more.

Sincerely,

Janis Wild, President
Wild-One's Good Idea Service

Figure 9.3    A successful response to an inquiry.

As you can see, the tone of the letter in Figure 9.3 is friendly, excited, and sincere.

The text of the letter answers all questions that the information request contained. It includes a sincere expression of interest and a minimum of "sell hype." Finally, the strong closing provides a good invitation to move the process along as the call to action in a delicate preliminary situation.

 **Sell Hype**    Sell hype happens when you are so obvious about pushing the strong points of your product or service that what you say sounds more like boasting than benefits for the reader.

## Using Form Letters

You may choose to use form letters for such situations as cover letters for routine matters, renewals, or answers to often-asked questions. In doing so:

- Be sure you maintain the feeling that one person is writing to another.

- Be sure the form letters you send respond to the interests of the people who will receive them.

- The content should be tested material from successful letters recently written.

In this lesson you learned guidelines and formats for writing effective informational memos and letters. The next lesson will be helpful if you need to deliver good or bad news.

# How to Write Good News Letters and Bad News Letters

*In this lesson you will learn several approaches to organizing and writing positive, mixed, and negative messages.*

## The Golden Rule for Good News and Bad

Before you write any message that delivers some kind of news and might inspire anxiety, sadness, or elation, pause and consider the golden rule for delivering good news and bad. Think from the point of view of the person you are writing to, and be considerate of his or her feelings in the way you deliver the message. For example, if you have to inform a consultant that you can no longer use his or her services due to budgetary constraints, take the time to praise his or her work to soften the blow, and offer to serve as a reference. Or, if the news you're delivering is good, congratulate the recipient for the personal or professional success.

# The Good News Is Easy

The contents of a good news letter often resembles the contents of an informational letter; the major difference is that when you write a good news letter, you have at least one benefit to offer your reader.

 **Benefit**   A benefit is something good the reader will get. To describe a benefit, take the reader's point of view and ask yourself what good the news in your letter would do for you.

In a good news letter, the benefit goes in your opener. Organize your letter exactly as you do for a letter of information, except the main point in your opener should be the main benefit:

- Begin with the benefit, and make it clear to your reader.
- Follow with well-organized details, explanations, and secondary benefits.
- Close with a request for action or friendly comment for goodwill.

Figure 10.1 provides an example of a good news letter, illustrating the organization described here.

---

Garland Yard and Garden Equipment

April 1, 1997
Mr. Robert Norbund
17 Window Road
Salient, Ohio 70994

Dear Mr. Norbund:

You'll be receiving a $475 refund check in the next few days and you can also keep the lawnmower, now that it's running well. This is not a customary solution for us, but your situation is also not customary.

We believe the blade bolt was damaged in shipping. It's not something easily detected, and it happens very rarely. It's unfortunate that it gave you so much inconvenience. We appreciate your patience. The enclosed refund, while not legally necessary, is meant as a gesture to compensate you for your trouble.

Now that the situation is corrected, we think you'll discover the quality advantages of our mower. We'd like to think that experiencing those advantages will lead you to our showroom once again in the future. In the meantime, happy mowing.

Best wishes,

Martin Garland,
Vice President, Customer Service

---

Figure 10.1    **A good news letter.**

There are no apologies in Figure 10.1, just an expression of empathy for inconvenience. This helps support the letter's assertion that the situation is rare. Avoid apologies and substitute statements that demonstrate you understand and empathize with your reader. The close is a friendly comment that reinforces the letter's goodwill gesture, combined with a gentle call to future action.

**Empathy**   Being empathetic or having empathy means being sensitive to another person's thoughts and feelings or putting yourself in that person's place.

## When the News Is Mixed

Mixed news usually combines bad news with some resulting benefits. To convey mixed news, use the same structure as in a good news letter.

But be aware that the benefit takes on an important strategic significance in a mixed news letter. The benefit must lead off your letter, as in the example in Figure 10.2, so that the bad news is not a major disappointment. It's essential to be positive.

TG&E

December 9, 1996
Lorraine Anderson
776 University Road
Sparta, IL 91900

Dear Ms. Anderson:

You will soon notice your telephone service is much faster, clearer, and less expensive than in recent years. Fiber optic and advance relay technology are coming to Sparta.

After three years of research and review of systems technology, TG&E has decided on an exciting course of action. We are going to pursue a technology that will handle the 24.8 percent population increase projected for Sparta over the next 20 years.

We know we can ask for your patience as we make the necessary changes to prepare for the future. At different times, different neighborhoods may experience occasional interruptions of service over a two-month period.

The actual interruptions may never occur. But, if they do, it will only happen once to any one neighborhood during our planned two-year transition. You'll be notified when your neighborhood's turn comes. We're confident you'll find that this small inconvenience in the present will have big results in the future.

We will make every effort to work efficiently and minimize interruptions. Can we count on your support? We've set up an information and suggestion line. Call toll-free 1-800-706-4458 to ask questions and make suggestions. We'd be delighted to hear from you.

Sincerely,

Wanda Tungsten
Senior Community Coordinator

Figure 10.2   **A mixed news letter.**

Pulling the benefit out from the negative news often takes strategic thinking. In Figure 10.2, the writer was told nothing more than that there would be interruptions in service and technical changes.

She had to discover what the changes would do for customers. She had to persist in asking questions until she found the angle that would show how an inconvenience can lead to a benefit.

If the writer had failed to find a benefit, she would have had to write a bad news letter.

# Writing a Bad News Letter

A bad news letter usually tells negative news and retains goodwill at the same time.

The only time this dual objective doesn't apply is when you want to be emphatic about the bad news and don't want to retain the reader's goodwill, as in a collection letter or a second refusal. The rest of this lesson assumes you want to retain goodwill.

> **!** **Write Carefully**   In business, you'll virtually always want to retain goodwill, because you never know when you may need to go back to a resource, or when your old employee may become your boss. Keep in mind that it's more difficult to convey empathy when you're writing instead of speaking, so phrase your bad news letter carefully.

In the following types of situations, you may find that you have to deliver bad news:

- Notifications of company policies that are not in the recipient's best interest.

- Notifications of a change in service or procedures.

- Refusals and rejections.

- Responses to complaints.

- Problems with an order.

- Problems with personnel.

## TWO STRATEGIES FOR ORGANIZING YOUR BAD NEWS LETTER

The way to determine your bad news letter's organization is to decide what comes first. Some people like to know the bad news right away, and others like to be softened a bit before they get hit. Some situations call for a direct telling of the negative message, and some for a little explaining before getting to the bad news.

Use the straight-to-the-point strategy:

- When you know the receiver well enough to know he or she prefers bad news first.

- When the situation is minor and the news would cause very little pain or disappointment.

- When your reader already distrusts you or your organization.

Here are the steps for getting straight to the point, as illustrated in the example in Figure 10.3:

1. Tell the news as directly as possible in your first sentence.

2. Follow with reasons that explain how and/or why the bad news happened.

3. Offer some alternative or compromise to the bad news if you can, or express optimism about a better outcome in the future.

4. Close with a positive statement, something aimed at soothing your reader's ego.

---

Whackville Travel Co.
May 2, 1996
Dennis Duolone
18 Crabwise Ave.
Ketchituri, MO 80909

Dear Mr. Duolone:

The airline won't refund your money. I'm sure you're not surprised. In the "Conditions" segment on the back of your ticket, they say no refunds for missed flights.

Sometimes they make exceptions, but only when life and death are involved.

Of course, your ticket is still valid. The best revenge might be to use it for a knock-out vacation.

We were happy to help you make your claim. It was worth trying. We would be glad to be of service again as your travel agent.

Regards,

Danielle Mason
Senior Service Officer

P.S. I've got some great suggestions for how to use that ticket. Stop in when you can.

---

Figure 10.3    **A bad news letter.**

> **tip**
>
> **Using P.S.** The use of a P.S. applies mostly to sales letter writing. But in letters where the tone can be light and all is not negative, a little sell can be successful. The P.S. is a good place to put the sell. It's separated from the body of the letter in a highlighted position.

The next approach, softening the blow, works best in most negative cases. (See Figures 10.4 and 10.5 for examples.) It allows you to get the news across without hurting the feelings of your reader. To use it, open your letter with what experts call a buffer.

A buffer is any kind of comment that evokes a positive feeling. For example, mention a past success, a minor benefit, a point of agreement between writer and reader, something that can be congratulated, or an expression of respect.

After the buffer, discuss the reasons for the bad news. Then tell the news.

Close with something to make the reader feel better if you have a good idea of what that might be. If not, be neutral and don't mention bad news again.

Don't close with this kind of statement: "We regret that we can't help you with your loss, but we wish you better luck in the future." Say instead, for example, "Perhaps, next time you'll be the winner, and we'll have an opportunity to congratulate you."

Knockworst's Sundries

August 20, 1996
Cerise Magnico, Chief Designer
WonderCreations, Inc.
18 Nickel Road
Angst, IN 60980

Dear Cerise,

You always plan the best events. You must get plenty of positive feedback. I hope this year won't be an exception.

Because of the tight timeline involved, I'm sorry to tell you we can't supply the custom decorations you requested. We called every supplier we know and none of them can do what you want in less than a month.

You can, however, get a standard decorative package on the same theme for the date you need it. I found a supplier with an idea you might like. The package won't have quite the flair you're noted for, but I believe you can use it as a base and build your style with accessory touches.

If this solution sounds feasible, call me. I'll come by with the catalog and we'll get the order in motion instantly.

Yours truly,

Robert Bellbottom
Chief Service Representative

Figure 10.4    One example of softening the blow.

State of Kentucky

April 24, 1996
Lester Wilson
Vice President of Marketing
Henderson Construction, Inc.
Palo Moto Road
Queendale, KY 34666

Dear Mr. Wilson:

Henderson Construction has a fine reputation and an impressive portfolio. We are glad you submitted a proposal for construction management on the new Aquatic Center job.

However, your price is in the higher range, and your availability is a bit too uncertain for this particular project. After a demanding review of all submitted proposals, we decided to award the contract to another company.

We are pleased that you were forthright about your limitations at this time, and we want you to know it will not hurt your chances on future projects.

We will be sending out RFPs for the State Finance Services Building in October. You're on our list, so hopefully we'll have another opportunity to do business together.

Good luck with your current projects.

Sincerely,

Chester Thorborough
Senior State Procurement Officer

Figure 10.5    Another example of a soft negative letter.

Note that in both of these softened letters, the letter started with a positive or neutral statement, used a bridge (explanation) to deliver the bad news, and closed with a positive.

## Ten Guidelines for Writing a Negative Letter

Finally, here are several more tips to keep in mind as you're delivering bad news. They will ensure that your message is straightforward, yet empathetic:

1. The key task of a negative letter is to gain acceptance for the bad news. Write from that point of view, as if you were seeking acceptance.

2. Don't go on about the bad news, but make it clear.

3. Don't place the blame on anyone. This is your opportunity to be impersonal and use the passive voice. For example, you can say, "The order was filled in error."

4. Be polite, clear, and firm.

5. Make the bad news seem reasonable.

6. Make readers feel they have been given serious and careful consideration.

7. Try to sound neutral or positive, if possible.

8. Keep the letter short.

9. The reasons you offer for the bad news should be business reasons, not personal.

10. Don't use "company policy" as a reason. It won't help with goodwill.

In this lesson, you learned approaches to organizing and writing positive, mixed, and negative messages. The next lesson explains how you can be persuasive in writing.

# 11

# How to Write a Letter That Persuades

*In this lesson you will learn how to make information persuasive, by appealing both to the rational and emotional aspects of each receiver's personality.*

## Persuasion Is Information with a Twist

Persuasion begins with real and reliable information. You won't persuade many people to do or to believe anything without some information to help them make a choice, or justify one.

Of course, there are techniques you can use to slant your information so as to persuade your reader to change a belief and even to act on that belief. You need to know and use these techniques to become an effective business communicator. After all, most job success depends on persuading others to try your approach, invest in a new product, choose your company, and so on.

But persuasion must walk an inexact ethical line. If you say anything untrue or conceal crucial information, you risk exposure and loss.

Use persuasion for requests, directions to others, team-building messages, recommendations for company action, sales letters, and anything else you write with the primary or secondary intention of influencing someone.

## THE BEST PERSUADER IS SOMETHING THAT BENEFITS YOUR READER

As always in good writing, you have to see things from your audience's point of view. But even further, to be persuasive, you have to identify conditions or items your audience would consider benefits.

For example, turning features into benefits is the cornerstone of persuasive advertising. For example, if you say your shovel has "an ergonomically designed handle," you've described a good feature. But to persuade someone to buy that shovel, you'd do better to tell them "the ergonomically designed handle will help reduce the risk of back injury." That's a benefit.

## THE RIGHT MIX OF REASON AND EMOTION

The two elements of a persuasive letter are:

- Logical reasons
- Emotional appeals

 **Emotional Appeal**   An emotional appeal is any statement intended to evoke emotional response. The appeal can be to sympathy, nostalgia, envy, greed, hero worship, fear of looking foolish, positive self-esteem, or any other normal human emotion.

Most of the time you need both logically solid arguments and emotional appeals that touch your readers. Used together, these two elements have a good chance of persuading your audience to action.

The balance between reason and emotion depends on four things:

1. What actions you wish to achieve.

2. Your readers' expectations.

3. The degree of resistance you must overcome.

4. How far you feel empowered to go in selling your point of view.

## WHEN REASON PREVAILS

Generally, lean toward logic and make your emotional appeal subtle when you are writing to persuade someone to:

- Accept a complex idea or recommendation.

- Take a very serious step.

- Make a large and important decision.

- Make a major purchase or donation.

Figure 11.1 provides an example of a letter that relies on logic and reason to persuade.

JS Consulting, Ltd.

May 29, 1996
Ed Wompetern, Director
Corporate Services
Wingnut Manufacturing
Rock Bottom Rd.
Nottingham Forest, GA 35612

Dear Ed:

I've examined your finishing procedures. You've done a fine job of honing them for lean, effective productivity. I think, however, that you can do more. I believe I have a solid recommendation for improvement.

If you put the burnishing procedure after the acid bath, you could completely eliminate the second polish.

As is, the acid bath follows the burnishing and undoes some of its desired effects. That's why you now need a second polish. Make the change and you'll save time, space, and work hours.

I know you face resistance from old-timers, but your savings in productivity will be worth the struggle. Why not present the change as a way to preserve jobs and salary increases. Tell them you're cutting procedures not people. It's true.

I urge you to suggest this change to your superiors. You can't lose, even if they deny it. And you deserve the credit. After all, it was really your idea for me to look in this direction. I only added the advantage of an outside eye.

I hope this has been helpful. If you need any kind of statistical projections, let me know, and I'll send you some hypotheticals.

Good luck and thanks for the opportunity.

Sincerely,

Syd Withall, Chief Engineer

Figure 11.1   A persuasive letter using logic and reason.

As in the example in Figure 11.1, a persuasive letter based on rational arguments opens with a direct statement of the subject, offers a sequence of strong arguments, anticipates opposing arguments, and offers a strong call to action.

Emotional elements form the persuasive letter's undercurrent. In Figure 11.1, the writer appeals to the reader's self-esteem and his worth in the eyes of his superiors. The writer keeps the tone of this appeal soft and friendly, and makes it secondary to his rational arguments.

## When Emotion Takes the Lead

Generally, lead with an emotional appeal and make the reasons support the appeal when you write a sales letter or a letter to persuade someone to join a cause or make a donation. Figure 11.2 shows an example.

As Figure 11.2 shows, letters based on emotional appeal begin with an attention-getter, establish a need, show how the writer can satisfy the need, visualize positive results, and make a call to action.

Reasoned arguments serve a secondary function in Figure 11.2. The writer simply asserts the benefit of using the new style of burnisher.

The letter sounds reasonable, but offers no concrete arguments to prove the value of the new style burnisher. None are really necessary since the writer simply wants to start the reader thinking about taking action.

Manufacturer's Association for Ending Wasted Motion

May 30, 1996

Ed Wompetern, Director
Corporate Services
Wingnut Manufacturing
Rock Bottom Rd.
Nottingham Forest, GA 35612


Dear Mr. Wompetern:

Suppose every ten minutes you had to put your arm in front of you, wave it back and forth three times, and then drop it to your side.

I'm sure you're familiar with the discomfort of repetitive motion. But wouldn't it be maddening if the repetitive motion accomplished nothing—if it were wasted motion.

Wasted motion is just what you have if you don't use a HydroPZ-Beta style burnisher for all metal fabrication finishing processes.

The patented HydroPZ-Beta process results in burnishers that solve the problem of lost luster after the acid wash. As a wingnut manufacturer, you certainly know the actual cost of correcting lost luster.

Imagine how happy your workers will be when you eliminate wasted motion, increase productivity, and raise wages.

There are presently four suppliers of HydroPZ-Beta style burnishers. Enclosed you'll find a list describing the suppliers and how you can contact them.

Please take advantage of this free information. Wasted motion is the enemy of productivity and healthy workers. Find out how much you can save while helping us to eliminate wasted motion in the American workplace.

Sincerely,
Ivan Jones, Association Director

Figure 11.2    A persuasive letter based on emotional appeal.

*tip*  **Sales Letters**  A sales letter would use the same structure as in the example in Figure 11.2. But it would put more emphasis on the features and benefits of a specific product. For example, a sales letter selling a specific wingnut burnisher might tell the reader how the burnisher achieves its motion saving benefits.

!  **Be Credible**  Always include details that communicate that you, your cause, your product, and your arguments are reliable. People judge credibility quickly, so be careful that your appeal does not endanger your credibility.

# PERSUASIVE STRATEGIES, APPEALS, AND TECHNIQUES

The following list is a sample of the kinds of persuasive approaches that have been tested and widely used. Be sure you know your audience before you use any of them:

1. Offer three to four good reasons that are meaningful to your reader.

2. Seek to be liked. Look for common bonds.

3. Use a positive appeal. Make your reader feel smart, generous, or perceptive, etc.

4. Use a negative appeal. Worry your reader about loss, missed opportunity, poor judgment, scarce supplies, etc.

5. Invite people to see themselves in a new light.

6. Present reasons and arguments taken from experts, and mention the experts by name.

7. Appeal to your reader's desire to learn.

8. Invite people to do something that accords with their known beliefs or past actions.

9. Make them feel a little guilty.

10. Lead with what sounds like a big request, and then make a smaller one.

11. Use a direct threat: "If you don't change we'll have to let you go."

12. Assume your reader will do what you want and don't offer any choices except for different ways to do what you want. For example, tell Mary how important she is to completing a certain project and then give her a choice of tasks she could do.

13. Ask your readers to imagine themselves in a situation that sets up your request or persuasive arguments. For example, "Suppose you had gone hungry when you were only five years old. Would you have prayed for help? Be assured someone is praying for your help even as you read this."

*tip* **Don't Leave Them Guessing** Once you make your persuasive arguments and appeals, be sure to make it easy for your audience to comply. Don't leave them guessing about what to do next.

# A CHECKLIST FOR AFTER YOU WRITE YOUR LETTER

After you write your persuasive letter, review it with the following questions in mind, and make any revisions as needed:

1. Have you made your desired result completely clear?

2. Are your arguments clear? Are they meaningful to your audience?

3. Is your emotional appeal consistent with the reasons you offer?

4. Have you worked inside your audience's frame of reference?

5. Have you been objective?

6. Is your tone right? Do you sound sly, evasive, exaggerated, cynical, angry, or insulting? Do you want to sound that way?

7. Have you taken account of the complexities of the situation you are addressing? The status of your audience? The circumstances that will influence your readers at the time of your letter?

8. Have you said anything untrue or concealed crucial information?

In this lesson you learned how to make information persuasive, using both rational and emotional appeals. The next lesson helps you evaluate your listening skills, which you'll need as others respond to your message.

# DEVELOPING YOUR LISTENING SKILLS

*In this lesson you'll learn good listening practices, pitfalls to good listening, how to be an active listener, and the benefits of active listening.*

## DID YOU CATCH THAT?

How often does poor listening make you miss an important point or phone number or botch a sale? It's important to be a good listener and to be perceived as one, since the communication process involves both sending a message and receiving feedback.

## SEVEN GOOD LISTENING PRACTICES

To improve your listening skills, consciously practice the following skills as often as you can. As you use the following techniques more often, they'll become more natural, although you'll still need to apply a conscious effort to maintain your listening abilities.

1. Focus 100 percent on the person speaking. Consciously show respect and consideration. Put the speaker at ease.

2. When your mind wanders, make eye contact with the speaker. Then shift focus and watch the words come from his or her lips. Repeat the words to yourself.

3. If you can take notes, train yourself to write everything down word for word. If you can't take notes, mentally identify main ideas and summarize them periodically.

4. Quiet your body and mind. Stop yourself from being preoccupied with anything but the matter at hand.

5. Keep yourself from mentally phrasing your response instead of hearing the speaker.

6. Delay judging what you hear until it's necessary. Suspend your own ideas and opinions until the speaker is finished.

7. Verify that you get what has been said. Remind yourself that the idea of good listening is to interpret the meaning of a message the way the other person intended. Ask questions to clarify points. Respond appropriately.

## HOW TO BE AN ACTIVE LISTENER

Active listening refers to a set of practices a listener can use to help understand the meaning of a speaker's message.

To be an active listener:

- Pay attention to how things are said, as well as to what is said.
- Listen for changes in the speaker's voice, tone, emphasis, pitch, or speed.
- Pay attention to the speaker's intention, as well as to what he or she says out loud.

- Listen for and differentiate between ideas, opinions, feelings, and facts.

- Work hard at perceiving the frame of reference and viewpoint of the person you are listening to.

- Work hard at understanding, as well as being understood.

- Put your understanding into your own words and use feedback.

## THE BENEFITS OF ACTIVE LISTENING

Active listening helps you take advantage of opportunities you might not otherwise notice. In addition, learning how to listen well to others earns you similar treatment from them.

Here are some benefits of active listening:

- Speakers feel less controlled by you and may release their feelings more easily.

- Speakers become less afraid of a negative response.

- Promotes more open relationships.

- Encourages speakers to keep communicating, to share more and go deeper.

- Facilitates working with others to solve problems and produce new understandings.

In this lesson you learned good listening practices, pitfalls to good listening, how to be an active listener, and the benefits of active listening. In the next lesson, you'll learn how your position within your organization affects the messages you send.

# 13

# COMMUNICATING WITH PEERS, SUBORDINATES, AND SUPERIORS

*In this lesson you will learn the formal norms of organizational communication, and how to communicate effectively with peers, subordinates, and superiors.*

## KNOW YOUR ORGANIZATION

Within the chain of command, your organization has written and unwritten rules about how individuals communicate with their peers, subordinates, and superiors.

 **Chain of Command** The chain of command consists of levels of authority from the top of the organization to the bottom. Each level has a reporting relationship with both higher and lower levels.

In some organizations, the most important rule is to follow the chain of command. In other organizations, there's greater flexibility, and you can communicate with someone higher in the hierarchy than your immediate superior as long as you send a copy of your message to that superior.

You need to know who gets hurt and who gets angry when you send a message that skips a level. In all cases it's important to understand how power affects the flow of information.

## POWER AND PERSONAL AUTHORITY

When it comes to the sharing of information within an organization, power means influence. Those with power can influence policy, planning, and operations.

But anyone who influences a decision, a project, a solution, or any daily activity has some power. The amount and kind of information you receive and send is directly related to your power.

Your power is defined by your place in the organizational structure and the culture of the organization. In terms of the written and unwritten rules of communication within the organization, your place determines what information others will share with you and who will share it.

An individual can add personal authority (sometimes called expert power) to his or her place in the hierarchy and therefore have more influence than normally goes with that place.

**Personal Authority**   Personal authority comes from having an established reputation as someone worth listening to and consulting.

You can achieve personal authority by being consistently knowledgeable about timely, crucial matters and by force of personality—from being a liked, supportive, and helpful person.

However, even those with personal authority beyond their place in the hierarchy should generally obey the established structure of their organization's flow of communication—or risk career consequences such as reduced effectiveness.

# Communicating with Peers

Good communication between peers is always important and especially so in team-oriented organizations. It's important for coordinating projects, producing well-executed, quality work, resolving misunderstandings, sharing insights, and support.

## Ten Good Habits for Effective Communication with Peers

It is best to assume that honest and open communication between peers is useful to you and your organization. Here are ten habits you can develop to build your effectiveness in communicating with peers.

1. Learn about each peer with whom you share information. Understand their attitudes and level of competence.
2. Establish trust. Don't betray confidences or volunteer a peer to handle undesirable projects, for example.
3. Play fair. This will go a long way toward giving you the right to expect fair play in return.
4. Find issues and activities related to work that interest you both. Find points of agreement about operational procedures. Share good ideas.

5. Show respect.

6. Talk willingly and don't hoard information once you establish trust.

7. Make solid and productive contributions to group projects.

8. Help others achieve their goals.

9. Help others develop their capabilities.

10. Give constructive feedback when appropriate.

## COMMUNICATING WITH PEOPLE WHO WORK FOR YOU

Your ability to communicate with the people who report to you is crucial to your success and theirs. You are accountable for bringing out their best, and they support you in meeting your responsibilities. Begin by knowing what most people want from their superiors:

- Information about how to do their jobs well.

- Information about the company.

- Explanation of team projects and how they relate to organizational goals.

- Constructive feedback on performance.

- Some degree of independence.

- Appreciation when they earn it, and without asking.

- A sense of belonging.

## Nine Ways to Develop Authority

To become more effective in communicating with team members who report to you:

1. Be fair and don't play favorites.

2. Be respectful.

3. Be as honest and direct as possible.

4. Be ethical about company business and flexible about individual problems.

5. Be clear about who is responsible for what.

6. Be empathetic and try to understand situations from their perspective.

7. Be aware of the emotional climate.

8. Be sensitive to the impact your messages have.

9. Monitor your nonverbal communication, particularly your tone of voice.

*tip*

**No Power Trips Allowed**   To earn respect and trust, minimize status. "Do it because I'm the boss" never motivates. Americans value the appearance of equality as well as actual equality. If you need to use your status to get things done, be prepared to handle some resentment.

## Giving Feedback

It's important to control your attitude when you deliver feedback, particularly to a person who reports to you. If you are highly judgmental, you will alarm your subordinate and make him or her defensive.

The most difficult task is to point out habits that harm performance. But if you do it right, by taking the following steps, you will be doing the person a favor:

- Plan exactly what you hope to achieve, think out what you want to say, and stay focused on performance.

- Choose a time when your own emotions are in control and your subordinate is not under unusual stress.

- Speak in private and choose your words carefully.

- Monitor your body language and tone of voice.

- Listen as well as talk.

> **!** **Remember the Goal**   If feedback gets out of hand, recall what you want to achieve before you talk. Be silent while you think. Remembering what you want to achieve will keep your emotions from deflecting you from your purpose.

## COMMUNICATING WITH SUPERIORS

When you want to communicate effectively with someone who has more responsibility and a higher position within your organization, start by taking your cues from established practice. If your superior really has an open door, then make use of it. If not, learn the acceptable way to approach him or her.

## WHAT DO YOU HAVE TO SAY?

Communication with superiors should be more formal than your communication with others. You can communicate about the following issues with your superiors:

- Information that directly serves your superior's decision-making duties.

- Ideas about specific projects.

- Important grievances and problems that would benefit from your superior's attention.

- Well thought-out suggestions for improving procedures.

- Established report information.

Avoid communicating about other issues that don't affect your performance, such as your personal relationships.

## HOW TO DEVELOP AUTHORITY WITH YOUR SUPERIORS

Of course, the first step to establishing a valuable reputation is to perform reliably and well. But that's just the first step. You also need to:

- Learn everything you can about your job, your department, your company, and your industry.

- Keep good notes in meetings and review them. You'll be valuable if you can help others remember what they accomplished and planned in meetings.

- Don't be shy about presenting your best ideas in high-profile settings, when you have your superior's attention.

- Be willing and ready to make your superior look good or help him/her when your team or department is in the spotlight.

- Find out what your supervisor thinks and what he or she needs to make decesions.

- Sharpen your timing so that you can alert your superiors to growing problems without the risk of giving bad news when it isn't wanted.

In this lesson you learned the formal norms of organizational communications, and how best to communicate with peers, subordinates, and superiors. In the next lesson, you'll learn how to demonstrate leadership in a meeting.

# 14

# COMMUNICATION AND PRODUCTIVE MEETINGS

*In this lesson you will learn the importance of communication in productive meetings, how to be an effective meeting participant, and how to be a successful meeting leader.*

## THE IMPORTANCE OF MEETINGS

Productive meetings keep an organization moving. Without skillful communications, meetings can waste time. They can set off an explosion of ideas, or provoke bad feelings, boredom, loss of face, or a sense of defeat.

### FORMAL AND INFORMAL MEETINGS, WRITTEN AND UNWRITTEN RULES

To establish order and fairness, large formal meetings use *Robert's Rules of Order*, which explain parliamentary procedure, and originated as the rules for carrying on debate and voting on issues in the British parliament.

If your organization uses Robert's Rules, learn them backward and forward. When you add that knowledge to the good verbal and nonverbal skills you learn in this book, you'll have a full guide to effective formal meeting behavior.

However, you're more likely to need to know informal techniques and procedures that make meetings productive and even enjoyable. Informal meetings are more of an everyday event. They're used for team building, problem solving, creative brainstorming, and information sharing.

## A GUIDE TO PRODUCTIVE MEETING PARTICIPATION

Get fully involved in the meeting so you can keep your mind constructively occupied.

When you get interested in the issues, it's easier to concentrate on the topic under discussion. You won't get preoccupied with the politics of the situation, your personal credibility, or your other work.

*tip* **Concentrate, Communicate**   Fire up all your communication and concentration skills for the face-to-face demands of a meeting. Use attentive body posture and gestures, an appropriate tone of voice, and active listening skills.

There are three rules of effective meeting participation:

1. Prepare before the meeting.

   • Read the agenda or find out the topics and goals.

- Track down any information you need to feel comfortable discussing the topics.

- Give thought to the people who will attend. Remind yourself of what you know about their styles of communication.

2. Be alert and constructive during the meeting.

   - Be flexible as well as alert.

   - Offer your prepared ideas only when they are appropriate and offer ideas that occur to you during the meeting only if you follow and understand the discussion.

**Keep Emotions in Check**   If your interest in a topic is emotional as well as intellectual, guard against bullying others with your point of view or interrupting the flow of the meeting to blurt out your feelings.

- Take good notes, especially if the meeting results in assignments.

- Maintain the tone set by the meeting leader.

- Don't put down anyone's ideas. Try to build on them.

- Don't dominate or take over the meeting.

- Unless time doesn't matter, don't divert the discussion.

- Don't dwell on a topic once the leader summarizes a sense of the group on that topic.

- When there are assignments or actions to be taken, volunteer.

3. Follow up.

   - Review your notes as soon after the meeting as you can.

   - Make a note in your calendar for all due dates assigned in the meeting.

   - If the material covered was complex or if you have any doubts about something you should know, contact someone else who attended the meeting and double-check your understanding.

   - Set a schedule for reporting to the meeting leader on your progress in assignments.

# A Guide to Productive Meeting Leadership

Meetings are productive when they carry forward the business at hand. Results aren't always measured by how much action the meeting produces. Measure results against objectives. A productive meeting fulfills the objectives of a well-planned agenda or a clearly stated purpose.

> **!**  **Time Is Money**  Meetings are a good place to remind yourself that time is money. Even when your objective is to help solve an emotional problem, there is a point where you are wasting time for all involved. Learn to stop before that point.

Good leadership practices for successful meetings include steps you take to prepare for the meeting, to lead the meeting, and to close the meeting.

## PREPARING FOR THE MEETING

Prior to planning the agenda:

- Make a list of everyone who should attend.

- Make a second list of all topics the meeting could cover.

- Put the lists aside and let the personalities and individual issues mix in your mind until it's time to plan.

When it is time to create the agenda, keep the following in mind:

- Consult your list of topics. Modify it according to ideas you've had since making the list.

- Note why you think you should include each topic. What's the goal? Information, brainstorming, discussion, or decision making?

- Don't try to cover too much.

- Consult your list of people who should attend and note which people are connected to which topics.

Then, to finalize the agenda, make a list of possible objectives for the meeting, and review the agenda with those objectives in mind, as follows:

- Unless circumstances dictate your objectives, choose only one or two.

- Make a final list of people and topics to suit your objectives.

- Put the topics in a logical order.

- Estimate how much time you need for each topic.

**Make the Most of Your Time**  Estimating time is a crucial skill. If you plan well you won't rush the issues or waste people's time. Meetings should be no longer than one hour unless circumstances demand otherwise.

- Schedule controversial items early and finalize the agenda.

- Distribute the agenda with related materials so people have time to review it before the meeting.

- Choose a meeting place to suit your objectives.

## CONDUCTING THE MEETING

Some simple steps can help you run the meeting effectively:

1. Start on time, follow your agenda, and end on time.

2. Get people to talk. Don't start with a statement of your opinion, or with a question that leads to an answer you already have in mind.

3. Don't dominate. Encourage participation. Be open and fair.

4. Seek information and opinions. Provide information. Offer your opinion once discussion is underway.

5. Clarify unclear comments.

6. Handle turn-taking. If a person at the meeting isn't speaking up, but you want that person's opinion, ask the person to respond.

7. Be courteous and firm handling disruptive behavior.

8. Be willing to deal with people's emotions and their level of involvement as well as the issues.

9. Integrate contributions to create a consensus. Restate the conclusion in a clear way.

10. Vote on your restatement of the consensus.

## CLOSING A MEETING

As meeting leader, you're also responsible for bringing the meeting to a clear, clean conclusion, as follows:

1. Summarize all decisions and remind the group who is responsible for what.

2. If there are no official notes taken, ask everyone to write down decisions and assignments.

3. Take more complete notes as soon as you leave the meeting.

4. Follow up within two to three days by confirming assignments with individuals and distributing minutes, notes, or promised materials.

In this lesson you learned how best to participate in and lead meetings. The next lesson focuses on more formal presentations.

# 15

# Making Effective Presentations

*In this lesson you will learn guidelines and tools for preparing and delivering a winning presentation.*

## Confidence Is the Key

The reason some people have an easier time with presentations than others is not that they're smarter or know more. They are just more confident.

That's the one secret of being a good presenter: You have to be confident to show confidence.

And what can you do to be confident?

1. Have faith in yourself. Tell yourself you can do it.

2. Do everything necessary to be well-prepared. Careful preparation provides the solid ground you need to support your self-confidence.

3. Know your audience and what you want them to get from your presentation.

4. Know your subject material and how to organize it for your audience.

5. Know yourself and how to project your best.

## ORGANIZE YOUR PRESENTATION TO REACH YOUR AUDIENCE

Use lists to get started and organized:

1. List all points you plan to cover.

2. Choose related points and put them in topic groups. Put them in order of importance.

3. Write your objective(s) at the top of the list.

4. With an eye on your objectives, make a priority list beginning with the most important topic groups.

5. Choose the five to nine topic groups you will cover. Set the list aside while you determine what format to use for your presentation.

## FORMAT YOUR PRESENTATION FOR EFFECTIVE DELIVERY

It's important to decide on your format before you begin creating the presentation. The format helps you shape your content as you begin to list topics and think about them.

1. Whenever possible speak from an outline.

   • Create the outline on paper and then put it on color-coded cards for delivery.

   • Put each topic group on a different color card.

- Write your main point at the top. Underneath, include brief reminder notes, supporting statistics, or quotes.

- If you're using slides or a presentation graphics program, remember to stick with one main idea and at most, a few bullet points per slide.

2. Plan for alternate lengths. Mark topics you can eliminate or add.

3. Use your outline as the basis for writing a formal speech.

When you have a written speech to deliver, use a marking system in the text to guide your delivery. For example, mark short and long pauses, word emphasis, voice variations up or down, louder or faster, softer, or slower, etc.

 **Formal Speech**   A formal speech is written out so that the speaker delivers full, carefully written sentences with deliberate word choices. Unless memorized, the speaker must deliver it by reading the text. An informal speech can be delivered from an outline, and the speaker doesn't have to worry about writing style or sentence structure.

## ORGANIZE THE CONTENT FOR DIRECT AUDIENCE IMPACT

If you've never written a presentation before, these techniques can help you organize:

1. Put your list of selected topic groups in the order that best achieves your objectives.

2. Set up a three-part outline: opener, body, and closer.

3. Plan a strong opening line.

 **Don't Worry About Humor**   In business presentations you don't have to entertain or open with jokes or anecdotes. Start out by getting to the point. Humor is O.K. if it arises out of the material, and if you feel easy doing it.

4. As you put your presentation together, keep in mind why the audience would want to hear what you have to say.

5. Complete the opener by telling the audience what's coming.

 **First Sentence Blues**   You don't have to start writing your presentation with the first sentence. Begin with the body. Fill in your ideas and comments for all the topic groups. Watch for the emphasis that emerges and for your best points. Knowing these things will give you ideas for a first sentence that leads into the body of your presentation.

6. Use your organized list of topic groups to outline the body of your presentation.

7. Remember, your audience is listening not reading. Use simple, familiar, understandable language.

8. If your objective is to inform, choose a strategy for organizing your sequence of points and topics. You can organize according to:

- A chronological sequence.

- Cause and effect.

- Problem and solution.

- A sequence of statements or descriptions.

- A story with a beginning, a middle, and an end.

9. If your objective is to persuade:

   - Begin with statements everyone would agree with.

   - Present a statement of your strongest argument.

   - Illustrate or expand on your argument.

   - Follow with a sequence of such statements and illustrations.

   - Know the arguments against your position, and without mentioning these arguments present answers that negate them.

   - Don't spend time on differences.

   - Summarize your main points before finishing.

   - Aim toward a final statement of what you want the audience to believe or do.

10. No matter what kind of presentation you give, make a clear break at the end. Your closer should be clearly a closer without having to say "in closing, I ...." Leave the audience with a strong argument, another startling fact, or a friendly summary.

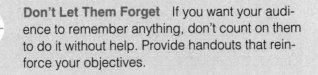

**tip**

**Don't Let Them Forget**  If you want your audience to remember anything, don't count on them to do it without help. Provide handouts that reinforce your objectives.

# FIVE GUIDELINES FOR PROJECTING YOUR BEST

Projecting your best means different things for different people, because we all have our unique strengths and weaknesses, but in general, giving attention to the following items will help you project your best:

1. Turn your nonverbal habits into good presentation habits:

   - Does your face reflect your feelings? Does it reflect what you are thinking? If it does, then all you need to do is concentrate on making your audience understand your material and your face will show that you sincerely want to communicate.

   - Can you stand straight without fidgeting, leaning, or slumping?

   - Can you look at the audience and only occasionally consult notes? You need to know your material so well that you're not dependent on notes.

   - Can you keep your voice calm and conversational *and* speak very clearly? Your goal is to speak fluently and fully pronounce your words. Don't slur or drop syllables.

   - Can you use hand gestures without being self-conscious? If hand gestures don't come easily, choose points of emphasis in your presentation and practice a variety of gestures until you find the ones that feel natural.

2. Project sincerity by believing in what you say and being as honest as you can be.

3. Project energy by being intensely involved with getting your points across.

4. Dress appropriately for the situation, eat normally but lightly, and get a little more rest than usual.

5. Control stage fright or simple nervousness, before and during presentation.

## HANDLING QUESTIONS

Listen carefully to questions. Don't avoid answering them or change the subject. A brief answer to the best of your ability will keep you in control even when your answers are not as good as you'd like them to be.

- Stay in your presentation made but be relaxed.

- Don't get into an argument or give anyone the opportunity to make a speech. Invite them to see you afterward.

- Try not to repeat yourself word for word.

- Tell yourself that your job in answering questions is to clarify your presentation.

In this lesson you learned guidelines and tools for organizing and delivering winning presentations. The next lesson helps you understand the power and meaning of nonverbal communication.

# Nonverbal Communication and Body Language

*In this lesson you'll learn the basic elements of nonverbal communication, suggested practices for sending the right nonverbal message, and good reasons to be aware of nonverbal signals.*

## The Nine Categories in Your Nonverbal Vocabulary

Even though you may not have considered them before, every day you use nine different types of nonverbal cues to communicate with others.

> **!** **Nonverbal Clues Tell the Story** Experts say the nonverbal portion of a message provides 70 to 90 percent of the meaning people draw from the message.

1. Facial expressions. Most of the time we automatically match our expression with what we say. But if you've ever been accused of an emotion you didn't

feel—looking impatient or angry, for example—you may need to think more about your eye and mouth expressions.

*tip*  **Cultural Differences**   While categories of nonverbal cues are the same in most all cultures, individual cues can have different meanings. A smile, a hand gesture, how close you stand—these and many other cues can mean different things than they do to Americans. See Lesson 18 for more on this subject.

2. Posture can indicate how you feel. Stand straight, stable, and balanced. Unless the situation is clearly informal, don't slouch. Lean forward to convey attentiveness. Don't cross your arms—it looks aggressive or defensive. Be careful of swinging your legs or tapping your feet. Both convey impatience.

3. Be aware of your gestures and movement. Hand and head gestures should complement or emphasize your verbal message. Open palms are positive, clenched fists are negative.

4. Be aware of the tone of your voice. Don't speak in a monotone. This bores people, and they will stop listening.

   - Seek variety in your tone from high to low. Suit the tone of your voice to your message.

   - Don't let your inflection take on a repetitious pattern.

**Practice Your Meanings**   Play with all the possible meanings you can give to a sentence. It will help you learn how to give the emphasis you intend to your message.

- Adjust your volume to suit your emphasis. Adjust your norm to a pleasing level and keep the variations for emphasis.

- Adjust the speed of your speech so that it conveys some enthusiasm.

5. Touch. In business situations, it's best to restrict yourself to a firm handshake for both men and women. If you want to show warmth or appreciation, do it in other ways besides touching.

6. Business dress. If your business has a clear dress code, then your choices are easy. If not, dress conservatively, and use common sense.

7. Surroundings and artifacts. Your office, workbench, or cubicle should communicate your interests and tastes without being distracting. Use common sense about the image you project.

8. Time and timing. Status controls time in the United States. Those who wish to demonstrate their superior position can keep others waiting. Those who emphasize productivity prefer punctuality. Consider punctuality the norm unless you know for sure that another standard applies.

9. Space. How close you stand to people communicates your degree of interest and involvement. Standing too close can be an offensive intrusion. Standing at a distance can look cold.

# FOUR GOOD REASONS FOR AWARENESS OF NONVERBAL SIGNALS

Even though you may think that worrying about nonverbal cues should be the least of your concerns, the following reasons may convince you otherwise:

1. You send nonverbal signals whether you want to or not. Without awareness you risk ambiguity.

2. When nonverbal messages contradict the verbal, most people believe the nonverbal.

3. If words and actions work together, you communicate your intended message the first time. If not, you give others reason to look beyond the immediate message for hidden information.

4. Nonverbal signals help determine the intensity of a speaker's feelings.

In this lesson you learned how to send the right nonverbal messages. Next, you'll learn about gender-oriented communication styles.

# 17

# GENDER-ORIENTED COMMUNICATION STYLES

*In this lesson you will learn differences between male and female styles of leadership, decision-making, work behavior, and habits of conversational behavior.*

## TWO CULTURES

Communication between the genders is similar to intercultural communication. Men and women have to actively find out about each other's frameworks.

## WHY IT PAYS TO UNDERSTAND GENDER-BASED STYLES

It always helps us interpret particular comments or actions made by a peer, superior, or subordinate if we know the frameworks that help shape the speaker's communications. Gender is one of those frameworks.

If someone of the opposite sex has a style of communication that seems puzzling, inefficient, or offensive, be sure you suspend judgment on that person until you take into account whether he or she is affected by habits of communication common to his or her gender.

For example, let's say a male employee knows that his female boss chooses to consider input from a variety of sources before making a decision. Knowing this, he is less likely to take offense or do something unnecessary when his input isn't put into action or when a decision seems delayed.

In fact, he might even speed up the process by helping to gather the input his boss wants for making what she considers a well thought-out decision.

Similarly, a female employee will be better able to take constructive action if she knows how her male boss communicates.

Let's say her boss makes decisions based on his own ideas plus what he absorbs by quick consultations with a few staff members. He consults but doesn't seek consensus. Knowing this, the female employee is less likely to take offense at being one of many who offer ideas without getting acknowledgment in return.

Begin with some knowledge of gender styles, and you won't automatically get defensive. You won't be tempted to interpret an unfamiliar approach to communication as impatience, disrespect, or a personal attack. You'll err only in the direction of being too tolerant. And that's not a bad way to go.

**!**   **No Stereotypes**   Avoid stereotypes. Be aware of how behavior is influenced by gender, but communicate with individuals. Don't make judgments based solely on current definitions of male and female styles of communication. And, be sure any characterization you make about gender is based on research, not old jokes and rumors.

# CURRENT DIFFERENCES IN STYLE

Research on male- and female-based behavior provides new information on gender comparisons almost daily. The following description of differences is based on conclusions widely accepted since the early 1990s.

Use these observations to sharpen your sensitivity, and keep current by being sensitive to the people you work with.

# STYLES OF LEADERSHIP

Generally, women prefer collaborative models of leadership and men prefer top-down models. The difference affects communication in the following ways:

1. Decision-making and the use of power. Women like to consult, gather information, and include many points of view before deciding what to do. Men like to get to the point, control the circumstances, and have power over other points of view to make decisions.

2. Women are more likely to scout. They compare, consider options, pause for reflection, and try to be sure all sources of information point to a good decision or approach.

3. Daily work behavior as leaders. Men are more likely to:

   - Choose a steady, continuous pace of action.
   - Prefer the active channels of communication (face-to-face and phone).
   - Not schedule time for planning and reflection.
   - Identify themselves by the jobs they hold.
   - Be reluctant to share information.

- Regard success as being at the top of the heap.

- View work as a means to an end, and therefore focus on completion more than on the actual doing of tasks.

Women are more likely to:

- Choose a fast and steady pace with scheduled breaks.

- Spend time on relationships important to achieving objectives.

- Consider it necessary to make time for activities not directly related to work.

- Prefer active communication channels, as men do, but make more time for mail.

- Identify themselves in more complex ways than job-defined.

- Regard success as being at the center of things rather than at the top.

- Take account of the larger context of work, and therefore focus on the process as well as the completion of tasks.

## STYLES OF CONVERSATION

Generally men prefer to stay focused on points directly linked and relevant to the discussion. They like evidence presented in statistics. Women prefer narratives that provide a background and context for the relevant points. They like case histories as evidence.

In terms of the use of verbal and nonverbal language:

- Men tend to use strong, direct language. They express hostility more. Women use more qualifiers, adjectives, and adverbs.

- Women tend to express preferences by asking a question. Men express preferences directly and are often blunt.

- Men tend to hear questions as direct requests for information. Women tend to hear questions as a way to keep conversation going.

- Women tend to use silence to respond to offensive comments, to express quiet disapproval. Men tend to think silence is a sign of appreciation or neutrality.

- Men tend to think nodding and smiling means agreement and approval. Women tend to nod and smile as encouragement, not necessarily as an expression of opinion. Men think an impassive expression is attentive and businesslike. Women think it is cold and disapproving.

> **!** **Don't Discriminate**   Be careful not to use language that discriminates on the basis of any category—not just gender, but physical characteristic, race, ethnic group, or age.

- Men sometimes don't look at a woman when talking to her. They address the woman by focusing strongly on a nearby man. Women sometimes refuse eye contact with men. They fear they will appear threatening and/or suggestive.

- Women are generally better at coding and decoding nonverbal messages. They hear a tone of voice and register changes in tone. Men don't notice, or they think that noticing is nit-picking.

- Men tend to be concerned with their appearance as an expression of power. Women tend to be more concerned with social pressures to be attractive.

With regard to conversational behavior, in meetings:

- Past studies show men interrupt more than twice as often as women do.

- Men speak more often and for longer periods.

- Men control the topics, and often don't respond to topics introduced by women.

In conversations between fewer people:

- Men see aggressiveness as a way to organize a conversation, to get things rolling. Women see it as negative and disruptive.

- Men respond to hearing a problem by offering advice and solutions. Women offer comfort and reassurance, except when openly asked for advice.

- Women prefer continuity from one comment to the next.

- Women prefer personal talk that seeks rapport. Men prefer impersonal talk that excludes emotion.

In this lesson, you considered differences between male and female styles of communication. In the next lesson, you will look at communication differences that exist between cultures.

# COMMUNICATING ACROSS CULTURES

*In this lesson you will learn guidelines for understanding how to communicate effectively with people from other cultures.*

## EITHER HERE OR THERE

Whether you do business internationally or in the United States only, your workplace is growing more multicultural.

## NICE GESTURE, WRONG CULTURE

When you interact with members of another culture, you can't just let good intentions rule your communications. You need knowledge of that culture as well as knowledge of the individuals involved. Let me illustrate from my own experience.

**Culture**  Culture means the customary conventions, attitudes, and behaviors of a group of people.

In 1979, the Japanese translator of my book about America in the 1960s came with his family to visit me and to see the United States. They arrived in a Wisconsin blizzard.

I had arranged housing, and to help them settle in I carried the largest pieces of luggage through the blizzard to the door. Beside me, the translator carried some smaller parcels, repeating in a barely audible whisper, "But you're older than I. But you're older than I." Japanese culture honors age. Americans take pride in youth and vigor. I had potentially embarrassed him because I was older, but I took over aggressively. And with the best of intentions, I performed the harder physical tasks. He had potentially embarrassed me by referring to my age as if I were too feeble to carry a bag even though I was bigger.

Fortunately we had established an individual relationship. Later we laughed about the number of personal insults involved in the incident.

## THE TWO MOST IMPORTANT GUIDELINES

The incident illustrates two essential starting points for communicating with people of other cultures:

1. Find out everything you can about cultural differences.

2. Always keep in mind that you are dealing with individuals. Some individuals may expect you to adhere to their cultural traditions to the letter. Others may take a more relaxed approach.

## SURE-FIRE BEHAVIOR WHEN YOU HAVEN'T HAD TIME TO FIND OUT MORE

There will be times when you can't do research about the cultures of those you're dealing with. What follows are the minimum standards you can fall back on in such situations:

1. Be respectful. People will more readily forgive mistakes if you feel and show respect.

2. Unless you know otherwise, tend toward the formal. Most countries value formality, particularly in business dealings.

3. Be alert and flexible about cultural differences. Keep in mind that your ideas about good behavior and values are influenced by American culture.

4. Be sensitive to other people, but don't take offense easily.

# FOUR GUIDELINES FOR INTERCULTURAL COMMUNICATION

Sensitivity to ethnic and cultural differences is necessary if you're going to avoid misunderstandings and promote collaboration.

To keep up with the flow of change, use these guidelines:

1. Respect your audience's cultural perspective. While they may be trying to blend into the American culture, they may still be confused about some issues, so treating them with consideration can only encourage good communication.

2. Share the work of communication. It's never good business to leave shared understanding to one party.

3. Watch for nonverbal signs of missed communication.

4. Be patient, but don't show it. Don't talk as if you were addressing a child.

# WHAT YOU SHOULD KNOW

To learn about a particular culture for use at home or abroad, focus on the following areas of cultural difference:

1. Styles of thinking. The mental frameworks and filters that individuals use to process information differ from culture to culture. Find out:

   - How the culture judges information: by logic, by gut feeling, by factual or scientific evidence, by gaining trust.

   - Whether individuals prefer generalizations, concepts, and abstractions, or concrete statements and agreements.

2. Primary values, ethics, and beliefs. The meaning of different forms of behavior also varies from culture to culture. Find out:

   - The norms of fairness and equality. Not all cultures believe in the ideal of democratic equality. Some have social and legal systems that rank people by gender, class, religion, ethnic, or tribal background.

   - The degree of emphasis on individual needs or community needs. Cultures vary in how they balance the rights of the community with the rights of the individual.

   - The degree of respect for authority. Don't assume that absolute obedience to authority is either proper or improper.

   - The degree of respect for competition. In the United States, competition is valued as a tool for shaping the marketplace to serve people's needs. In some cultures, competition is viewed as harmful to ethical behavior.

- The degree of respect for efficiency. In the United States, the most efficient course of action is frequently considered the best. In some cultures efficiency is less important.

3. Protocol and norms of business practice. Most of us accept certain conventions of business behavior and dress without much thought until the conventions are violated. Violations of convention are a negative distraction in any culture, no matter how small or large their importance. Find out:

- Forms of address. Use appropriate titles and forms of greeting.

- Decision-making conventions. Do individuals make decisions, or are groups also involved?

- Conventions of negotiation. Must agreements have a personal side? How are offers made and accepted?

- Attitudes toward punctuality. The norms of appointment scheduling vary. Determine if punctuality is proper, and if not, how early or how late is polite.

- Attitudes toward gifts and entertaining. Are gifts expected or offensive? If the occasion arises, how formal or informal should dining or socializing be?

4. Religious rules that affect business. Some cultures do not separate religion and social order. Business, like everything else, must conform to holidays, food requirements, and conventions of religious observance.

5. Language. It's to your advantage to know the language of any culture you do business with, even when English is the official language of communication. Find out:

- How to say such courtesies as: "thank you," "please," "good morning," etc. This is the minimum you should do to acknowledge your audience's language.

**Use an Interpreter**   If you are not fluent in a negotiating partner's language have an interpreter with you. Choose one who is also aware of nonverbal signals and negotiating styles for the negotiating partner's culture.

- What is the appropriate conversational style. How fast should you talk? How slow? What tone of voice is appropriate and what meaning do different tones carry?

**Avoid Slang**   Avoid using contractions, slang, and metaphoric language, such as figures of speech from sports or literature.

- What is a compliment and what isn't. Determine how to respond to compliments and how to extend them.

- How to present benefits or negative news. How direct and how frank should you be?

6. Nonverbal communication. Even small hand gestures or body postures could vary in meaning from culture to culture. For example, the American thumbs-up gesture is offensive in several cultures. Find out:

   • Differences in facial expressions, gestures, body language, styles of walk, eye contact, touch, and use of space.

   • Attitudes toward action and silence. Is there a right time to be quiet? Does silence signal disapproval or interest?

   • The meaning of a smile. Should you smile at strangers, for strategic reasons, or to cover embarrassment?

   • Attitude toward emotion. Tears and anger are generally taboo in business, but acceptance of other emotions varies from culture to culture.

   • Symbolic meanings. Colors have different meanings in different cultures. So do height, size of an office, style of dress, and age.

In this lesson you learned guidelines for understanding how to communicate effectively with people of other cultures. Next you'll learn more about a facet of your organization's culture: the grapevine.

# 19

# UNDERSTANDING AND USING THE GRAPEVINE

*In this lesson you will learn what the grapevine in your organization is, how it operates, and how you can make use of it.*

## THE GRAPEVINE GROWS EVERYWHERE

No matter which formal pattern of communication your organization uses, you can be pretty sure the informal "grapevine" also exists.

The grapevine offers people an unofficial information exchange where they can share their own interpretations of organizational events, personalities, and policies.

The grapevine can also be a "gripevine," giving participants relief from stress by offering an outlet for complaints.

## WHERE DOES IT COME FROM?

Information begins travel on the grapevine whenever work mates talk about what's happening on the job. If circumstances in an organization promote the spread of speculation about any issue at all, people will pass on what they hear and think.

The grapevine is also kept busy by overheard comments, insider information from executive assistants and secretaries, or faxes read by unintended receivers.

## AND WHAT DOES IT SAY?

The topics most frequently discussed on the grapevine include:

- Changes in company policy and organization.
- Potential hirings and firings.
- The organization's fortunes, good or bad.
- Production problems, bottlenecks, and poor procedures.
- Who's in power and who's out.
- Who's looking for another job.
- Who gets paid how much.
- Sexual harassment information.
- Union activities.
- The boss's style of managing.
- Gossip about people.

## A BUSY GRAPEVINE CAN LEAD TO MISINFORMATION

The grapevine adds a potentially vital dimension to an organization's flow of information. What people say informally is usually more open and direct, and therefore can be useful for improving organizational performance.

It's also normal for the grapevine to grow and shrink like a shadow, as the organization moves. But when the shadow begins to move on its own, something is wrong.

Grapevines are most active during periods of change when people experience their highest levels of fear. Fear gives the exchange of information extra intensity, and it makes distortion very likely.

If an organization does not keep its employees well informed during periods of change the grapevine may take off on its own.

# What You Can Learn From the Grapevine

Aside from the plain fun of social interaction, you can use the grapevine to:

- Identify problems.
- Be alert to current changes.
- Learn the working style of your superiors.
- Discover a better, faster, or easier way to do a task.
- Determine the mood of the work force.
- Find out what information is being distorted.
- Learn who to believe, who to trust, who's informed and who isn't.

> **!**   **Verify What You Hear**   Watch out for exaggeration, especially if your organization does not keep its formal channels of information open. Keep in mind that the grapevine carries speculation as well as information. Always consult as many sources of information as you can before forming an opinion. Your superior might even welcome a direct question.

# COUNTERACTING FALSE GRAPEVINE NEWS

If you know false rumors are flying, and you are in a position of responsibility, act promptly to counteract false rumors:

- Tell your concerns to your superiors.

- Encourage or initiate memos, meetings, newsletters, and bulletin board announcements to deal with the false news.

- Talk about it with your grapevine mates.

In this lesson, you learned how to make use of the grapevine. Next, you'll learn how to apply your communication skills to manage disagreements.

# - 20 -

# Using Communication Skills to Solve Disagreements

*In this lesson you will learn how to use communication skills to identify problems that underlie disagreements, how to pursue solutions when others disagree, and what to do when others disagree with you.*

## Solving Disagreements Between Others

Disagreements are not always a matter of poor communication. Some grow from misunderstandings, and some from mismatched expectations. But, many are the result of real differences between individuals.

Nonetheless, even in cases of disagreement, a good communicator can help avoid a destructive conflict. The result could even be a solution stronger than any of the conflicting positions.

# IS THERE A SERIOUS PROBLEM?

Here are four signs of a serious problem:

1. The conditions are right: there are genuine personality differences, the times are tense from extra work or failed support, a provocative issue is on the table.

2. Two or more people are more easily inflamed than usual.

3. Two or more people show signs they are feeling unfairly treated.

4. Two or more people begin directly or indirectly accusing each other of one thing or another.

# FIND THE SOURCE OF THE PROBLEM

Once you know there is a problem to solve, meet with the individuals involved and find out each person's version of the problem and issues. Use the following techniques to research these opinions:

- Leave plenty of time so you can let people talk it out without feeling rushed.

- Make it an informal meeting. Pick a neutral, comfortable setting. Use relaxed and friendly body language.

- Explain that your purpose is not to assign blame. Your job is to find a solution that puts an end to the threat and, hopefully, satisfies all parties.

- To be clear about the problem, ask leading questions and use your active listening skills. Don't show approval or disapproval.

- Look past the presentation of the problem to see what each party really wants. They may be stating the problem incorrectly. Restate it for them and ask if solving that particular problem would bring the matter to a satisfactory end.

# WHAT TO LEARN FROM MEETING WITH INDIVIDUALS

To equip yourself with an understanding of the disagreement be sure to gather the following information:

1. All versions of what caused the dispute.

2. All versions of what provokes the difference of opinions.

3. The points of agreement between the parties involved, their common ground, and the assumptions they share.

4. Each person's expectations for how the situation that caused the disagreement should have been handled.

5. The assumptions that underlie each person's expectations.

6. What triggers emotions for each individual.

7. Each person's opinion of the other (or others).

8. Each person's awareness of the problem's impact on the organization.

9. What each person thinks would solve the problem.

10. Which individuals want to solve the problem and which want to prove they're right.

# TAKE SOME TIME TO PUT THE PIECES TOGETHER

After you've met with each individual, take time to prepare for a meeting between all parties.

- Check the accuracy of everyone's information.
- Sort out the grounds for agreement.
- Search for alternatives.

# CHOOSE A STRATEGY

If you need to bring the involved parties together for face-to-face negotiation, choose a strategy before you meet. You can take three approaches:

1. The old organizational style is to force the parties involved to find a solution or accept one that you impose. Experience shows this is a fast technique, but the solution is not long lasting. Use it only when you have absolutely no other choice.

2. The logical solution is a compromise. If you asked the right questions in your individual meetings, you'll know if the disagreeing parties will accept a compromise.

3. The optimum solution is a full resolution of the issues involved. This means you bring the parties together and work together on the solution. You find exactly what each values and how it can be achieved to everyone's satisfaction.

# Bring the Disagreeing Parties Together

For the face-to-face negotiation session, set the scene carefully. Choose a time and place agreeable to all. Define some ground rules, such as: hearing each other out with no interrupting, talking directly to each other, being frank, and agreeing to focus on a solution.

Use these tactics to guide the negotiation session:

1. State the problem in neutral rather than emotional terms.

2. Be concrete.

3. Don't talk in terms of personalities.

4. Don't make absolute statements.

5. Demonstrate your confidence that the disagreeing parties can resolve their differences.

6. Ask open-ended questions that require explanations.

7. Get all parties to express their idea of the problem.

8. Get all parties to hear the other version and repeat their understanding of it.

9. To keep things moving, ask questions that help them recall what they said in the individual meetings.

10. Set the tone with a calm manner and friendly facial expressions.

11. Be aware that everyone risks loss of face. Make it your job to see that everyone involved saves face.

12. Lead people toward the points of agreement or common ground you discovered in the individual meetings.

13. Keep people away from tangents.

14. Look for statements that open a door to conciliation.

15. Don't quit until some kind of agreement is reached and stated out loud.

## IF THE DISAGREEMENT IS WITH YOU

If the dispute results from others on your team disagreeing with your point of view, you should:

1. Treat the disagreement as constructive criticism.

2. Find out the real concern of your critic.

3. Check for feelings, to understand critic's unspoken emotions and ideas.

4. Re-examine your position.

5. Restate any part of the criticism you agree with.

6. Let your critic respond next.

7. Reassert what you still believe, but don't justify it. Don't be defensive.

8. Show your willingness to listen and consider what is said.

9. Be willing to find mutual ground as quickly as possible.

10. If the disagreement is not resolved to your satisfaction, ask for time to think over the criticisms and meet again. Then prepare to seek common ground in the next meeting.

In this lesson, you learned how strong communication skills can help achieve fast, effective resolutions to disagreements. The next lesson explores how to evaluate your success as a communicator.

# Measuring the Effectiveness of Your Communications

*In this lesson you will learn how to seek and make use of feedback on your effectiveness as a communicator.*

## Time to Face the Music

You are responsible for how successfully you communicate. This is true even when you operate within narrow organizational limitations. Such limits can't completely stop a clear communicator from being effective, and they can't serve as an excuse for a poor communicator.

## Sensing Feedback and Using Feedback Systems

There are two methods for testing how well you communicate. You can develop a sense of how you're received, and you can develop a system to measure if your communications are doing what you want them to do. It is clearly beneficial to develop and use both methods.

## SENSING SUCCESS AND FAILURE

To develop sensitivity in face-to-face communications, you can use your active listening skills and your ability to read nonverbal signs to determine how your listeners are responding.

In written communications, you can learn to read between the lines of responses to your messages.

Choose someone you communicate with regularly, someone you trust, and ask for a critique. The more clearly you demonstrate that you seriously want to know how to improve, the more thoughtful the response you will get.

# HOW TO CUSTOMIZE A MEASUREMENT SURVEY

To make a personalized survey that helps you evaluate your performance as a communicator, review this book and choose the principles you most want to master. Then simply turn them into questions.

For example, you might ask if the information in your messages is accurate, well-organized, and relevant. You might ask if your point of view gets in the way of productive communications.

In fact, you could construct all of your survey questions from Lesson 22. However, if time allows you to be more complete, you should draw questions from other lessons that cover situations particularly relevant to you.

Make your survey formal or informal depending on whether communication skills are central to your job. If they are not central, you should make the survey short and informal.

## SOME SUGGESTED MEASUREMENTS

The value of a survey is that it makes patterns emerge, and the patterns offer convincing evidence of what you need to change.

Construct a questionnaire to help you determine if people feel:

- It's easy to approach you.
- You treat everyone as equals and with dignity.
- You usually communicate through the right channel.
- You send enough memos and e-mail, and have enough personal contact.
- Your body language, facial expressions, and other nonverbal signals serve you well or poorly.
- You listen well.
- You are easy to understand when you speak and write.
- You avoid clichés, jargon, stock phrases, and other causes of misunderstandings.
- You are comfortable with cultural- and gender-based differences, and you communicate well with diverse people.
- The content of your messages is usually interesting and reliable.
- You time your messages well.

## KEEP AT IT

Once you get answers to your survey questions, you may still have even more specific questions to ask. Do some self-analysis before you ask for any more feedback.

It's important not to be discouraged. If you review the lessons in this book periodically, you will develop the habits you want. Believe it and try.

Being a good, clear communicator is one of the most demanding skills in the range of human activities. Just about everyone needs to learn how to be good at it, and just about everyone can.

In this lesson you learned how to seek and make use of feedback on your effectiveness as a communicator. The next, and final, lesson helps you explore techniques you can employ to avoid future misunderstandings.

# 22

# Avoiding Misunderstandings in Communication

*In this lesson you will learn steps to help you use the elements of the communication process to prevent problems that get in the way of shared understanding.*

## Who Is to Blame?

Misunderstandings in business can be worse than frustrating. They can sabotage productivity and reflect badly on all involved.

Placing the blame wastes time that is better spent fixing the problems. The best way to deal with a misunderstanding is to prevent it before it happens.

The five causes of misunderstanding are verbal, nonverbal, interpersonal, organizational, and cultural.

## Keys For Preventing Misunderstanding

Here are some ways to deal with the causes of misunderstanding.

1.  Verbal. To eliminate a verbal problem that could cause a misunderstanding:

- Avoid poor pronunciation and careless articulation.

- Be aware of your knowledge level and the level of your listeners.

- Improve your vocabulary. Using a big word doesn't show an extensive vocabulary. Using the right word does.

- Don't use poor grammar. You will be misunderstood and judged poorly if you make basic errors such as using a plural subject with a singular verb.

- Purge your talk of slang, jargon, and euphemisms.

- Minimize abstractions. Abstractions refer to anything that can't be touched, tasted, seen, smelled, or heard.

- Eliminate ambiguity. Be exact in your choice of words.

- Don't use clichés and stock phrases. Clichés and stock phrases turn off involvement.

2. Nonverbal. The source of a misunderstanding may be a nonverbal cue you're giving. Make sure you:

  - Eliminate inappropriate signals. Giggling at a serious comment is inappropriate.

  - Eliminate conflicting signals. Smiling and nodding your head while you say negative things sends a conflicting set of signals.

  - Be alert to differences in interpretation. Check with co-workers to see how they interpret documents and memos. Ask others to tell you what they heard in a meeting to see if you heard the same things.

  - Monitor your emotional involvement. Sometimes excitement or anger is exactly what you want to communicate. But your emotion is excessive if it takes the focus away from what you are saying.

- Be aware of distractions. Don't try to talk over something that is distracting your audience. If there is noise outside the door or a private conversation right in the same room, acknowledge what's happening.

  If you see your audience focusing on your gestures, or on how close you are standing, back off. Then repeat what you've just said in a friendly way to help your audience pick up what you were saying before they were distracted.

- Practice the skills of good listening. Listening is important to effective communication.

3. Interpersonal. Relationships between people color all communications:

   - Don't stereotype your audience.

   - Don't let role-playing define your communications.

   - Don't assume your audience shares your point of view.

4. Organizational. The structure of your organization may cause misunderstandings by creating such barriers to communications as: job specialization, hierarchical structures, impersonal standards of behavior, work overloads, information hoarding, or information bottlenecks. There are two things you can do to deal with these barriers:

   - Be patient, play by the rules, and be as clear as you can be within those rules. If you break the rules, your communications will be completely disregarded. If you are patient, you stand a better chance of having other people listen to you.

- Avoid being influenced by cliques and in-groups. They usually exist for social reasons, for prestige, or for an outlet to complain about the company or the boss. Information from these groups is always slanted.

5. Cultural. As with male/female relationships, cultural differences provide a minefield of potential misunderstandings. See Lesson 18 for keys to communicating across cultures.

## MAKING SURE YOUR MESSAGE HITS THE MARK

No matter how much you pay attention to the preceding suggestion for preventing misunderstandings, you also need to examine the message itself to ensure it's not the source of any failure to reach common understanding. The techniques listed in the rest of this lesson can help you ensure your message achieves your communication goal.

1. Check the message information. Make sure the information in your message is accurate, well-organized, and relevant.

- Double-check facts.

- Make an outline of what you want to say or write.

- Eliminate irrelevant information.

- Eliminate information overload.

2. Choose your channel carefully. Think about what is the most appropriate way to convey your message: face-to-face, by phone, e-mail, personal memo,

general memo, or statement for everyone to read. The more complicated or ambiguous your message, the more likely face-to-face communication will work best.

3. Be aware of your environment. Make things comfortable and place yourself in a strong position of focus for your audience.

4. Examine your own point of view. Your personal point of view can create habits of thought that affect the value of your message. Ask yourself if the following habits are limiting your effectiveness.

   • Do you automatically put information into familiar categories?

   • Do you let past experiences irrationally affect what you think will happen in the future?

   • Do you have prejudices about the information you want to send?

5. Keep the message goal in mind. Keeping the purpose of your message in mind will help you avoid the following obstacles to clarity:

   • Trying to impress instead of making genuine contact.

   • Making hidden assumptions about what your audience knows or needs to know to understand your message.

   • Making leaps in logic so that the connections between your statements are left unsaid. Perhaps you hear the connections in your mind, but others see or hear only separate, unconnected statements.

- Using "either/or" thinking to classify all problems as having only two possible solutions, allowing for no alternatives or middle ground.

*tip*    **Keep Notes on Yourself**   Start a self-knowledge notebook and jot down instances where you can improve your mental habits, knowledge of your audience, and your techniques of good listening.

6. Understand how company culture affects communication openness. Some company cultures do not foster openness. Work within the limitations and the politics of your company culture.

7. Learn how to communicate with different levels of the hierarchy. You need to know what style, behavior, and level of frankness is appropriate and expected in dealing with superiors, subordinates, and peers.

8. Know your receiver or audience. Sometimes this takes no more than pausing to reflect on what you already know. Sometimes it takes conscious analysis.

9. Encourage frank feedback. If you want your communication to survive the basic complications of the process and succeed, find ways to learn what your audience thinks you are saying.

10. Learn techniques of good listening. Begin by simply reminding yourself not to be thinking about other things when you should be listening.

In this final lesson you learned steps you can take to review your communication habits and messages to ensure that your communication skills become more effective.

# INDEX

## A-B

agendas, meetings
  conducting, 81-82
  planning, 80-81
audiences
  analyzing, 12-13
  difficult messages,
    16, 20
  intercultural
    communication, 105
  miscommunication,
    preventing, 123
  multiple, 17
  nonreceptive, 14-16
  presentations, 83
    *organizing, 84*
  reaching, 13
  targeting, 14
  writing, 29
authority, establishing
  cultural perceptions,
    103
  personal, 69-70
  receiver complications,
    7

## C

chain of command, 68
communication, 2
  channels
  (communication)
    *appropriate, 19*
    *combining, 22*
    *complications, 6-8*
    *gender preferences,*
      *96-97*
    *types, 6-7*
    *see also speaking*
  conversational, 2, 99
  effective
    *defined, 1*
    *importance, 3*
    *measuring, 117-120*
  forms, 2
  gender-based, 19, 94
    *differences, 96*
    *research, 96, 99*
    *stereotypes, 95-96*
  informal, 107-109
  intercultural, 100-106
    *misunderstandings,*
      *avoiding, 102,*
      *121-124*

persuasive
*necessary elements,*
*57-62*
*samples, 59-62*
*writing effective, 64*
positive samples, 45-47
sales, 62
listening, 65
active listening, 66-67
*benefits, 67*
avoiding misunder-
standings, 123
measuring skills, 118
resolving conflicts, 112

# M

measuring skills, 118
meetings, 18
closing, 82
conducting, 81-82
formal, 76-77
gender-based
communication
differences, 99
informal, 76-77
leadership, 79-80
preparing for, 80-81
productive participa-
tion, 77-79
resolving conflicts,
112-113
memos, 18
preventing
misunderstandings,
122

samples, 40-43
writing effective, 39
messages
complications, 6
e-mail, 33-37
goals
*analyzing, 9*
*identifying, 10*
*understanding,*
*10-11*
letters, 39-43
*mixed, 47-49*
*negative, 49-55*
*positive, 45-47*
memos, 39-43
nonverbal
*cultural differences,*
*91-93*
*gender differences,*
*98-99*
*importance, 93*
*types, 90-93*
preparing
*gathering facts, 24*
*necessary tools,*
*25-26*
*reviewing, 26-27*
timing factors, 22
*see also* audiences
misunderstandings
causes, 121
preventing, 121
*intercultural, 124*
*interpersonal,*
*123-124*
*nonverbal, 122-123*